Test, Evaluate and Improve Your Chess

A Knowledge-Based Approach

by
IM Dr. Danny Kopec
and
NM Hal Terrie

June, 2004

To: Nicholas Trieu,

A serious chess student!

USCF Press, New Windsor, New York

Best Wishes,
IM Dr. Danny Kopec

Test, Evaluate, and Improve Your Chess: A Knowledge-Based Approach
© 1997, © 2003 by Danny Kopec and Hal Terrie

First edition published by Hypermodern Press, 1997
Second edition published by U.S. Chess Press

Editor: Glenn Petersen
Book design & typography: U.S. Chess Federation, USCF Press:
Jami L. Anson, Claudia Bonforte, Jean Bernice,
Cathy Garone, & Paula Helmeset
Cover Design: Claudia Bonforte
Cover Photos: Jami L. Anson, Claudia Bonforte
Graphics: Claudia Bonforte, Kathleen Merz
ISBN: 0-9700852-1-4
Library of Congress Card Catalog Number: 96-076190

Printed in the United States of America
1   3   5   7   9   10   8   6   4   2

To my parents,
Magdalena and Vladimir Kopec,
for their support.

— D. K.

To Charles Baden,
who taught me most of what
I know about chess.

— H. T.

Contents

U.S. Chess Federation's mission statement

USCF is a not-for-profit membership organization devoted to extending the role of chess in American society. Founded in 1939, USCF promotes the study and knowledge of the game of chess, for its own sake as an art and enjoyment, but also as a means for the improvement of society. The USCF offers a monthly magazine, various other publications, and organizes many chess tournaments, bestowing national titles. USCF offers discounted chess books, products, and provides many other benefits to its more than 90,000 members. We serve as the governing body for chess in the United States and as a participant in international chess organizations and projects.

845.562.8350 Fax 845.561.CHES (2437) 1-800-388-KING (5464)
www.uschess.org
3054 US ROUTE 9W, NEW WINDSOR, NY 12553

Introduction

By IM Dr. Danny Kopec

You might ask: Who needs another chess quiz or test book? So many excellent ones have been developed over the years; why should this one be necessary or be better than any other? My answer is another question: How many relatively small (24-position) test sets do you know which can pinpoint your chess strength in about an hour? Very few, and that is because too little thought has gone into determining the very specific components that comprise chess strength. There are many books which specifically test tactical motifs, in which you have to find all kinds of mates, and which test your ability to find forcing solutions to endgame positions or studies, but few which try to test and expand your knowledge in a holistic way. Furthermore, most tests are concerned with moves. In this book we will also be concerned with moves, not as ends in themselves, but rather as symbols for concepts or chess knowledge which can be represented by a move, sequence of moves, or pattern. Moves can be viewed as steps in a larger procedure which represents a plan or a grand theme. Hence our subtitle: a knowledge-based approach.

I feel that the attraction of chess is that it is one of the few arenas of life where you can, (and must) detach yourself from all the other demands of life just to think and compete. In playing chess we are betting on (or applying probabilities to) the value of our knowledge. Every move of every chess game is in effect such a bet. Two players share their knowledge on the chessboard and embellish it with calculation, bringing about a merciless struggle to achieve victory.

We often come across phrases in literature like conducting an attack or orchestrating an attack. Chess allows each one of us the opportunity to become conductors and orchestrators of forces, even though we may never have entered an orchestral pit, and have no formal training as conductors.

That is the allure of chess. A fantasy world where humans quietly interact, compete, and discuss ideas, leading to great tension in the struggle to achieve victory and avert defeat.

The roots of this book began in 1980 when I developed a set of test positions with my then colleague, Dr. Ivan Bratko of the Machine Intelligence Research Unit of the University of Edinburgh. Our unit was headed by Professor Donald Michie. The idea was to demonstrate that computer programs lacked certain knowledge which is critical to strong chessplayers and is necessary for their advancement to the master level. During that time period much discussion centered around the relative merits of brute force methods versus selective search or heuristic methods. The 24-position test we developed became known among computer chess researchers as the Bratko-Kopec Test (BK-Test). This test was a standard for well over a decade in measuring the progress of computer chess programs. Many developers of computer chess programs (both commercial and academic) have used the concept of levers embodied in this test to improve their programs' pawn play, thereby bringing about a more sound strategical approach. The test has also proven extremely reliable as a way of measuring chess strength both for humans and computer chess programs. That is, your rating can be used to predict your score on the test, and your score on the test can be used to predict your rating. The test has been administered to many human chessplayer subjects in various places around the world where I have lived including: Edinburgh, Scotland (1980-82), Montreal, Canada (1983-84), San Diego, California (1984-86), Orono, Maine (1986-92), Ottawa, Canada (1992-93), and at my summer Chess Camp in Pomfret, Connecticut (1994-95), London, England (1997-99), Long Island, New York (1999 - present), and our Summer Chess Camps at the Lawrenceville, School, 1997 - present.

During the course of these years the test has been administered in a number of forms. Even as early as 1980 we were able, with the help of a technician, to work with a chess TV-display monitor. The monitor was about 13 inches in size and facilitated administration of the test to about five people at once. In the early years, very eager to collect data for publication purposes, I would often administer the test to one person at a time, two minutes per position, 24 positions, multiple subjects being tested individually. This would easily take me many hours. Later we moved on to test booklets with each position diagrammed on a separate sheet. Here, had my research not been conducted at universities, the photocopying costs would have been prohibitive. A cheaper but more clumsy and tedious form of test administration made use of chess demonstration boards. During the past 10 years or so, I have been able to test an entire class at once by using a laptop and a computer projector, and this too has been very effective for our camps.

In this book we make these tests available to the general chessplaying public. You have an opportunity to take and score yourself on seven tests which have been specifically designed for you. We believe that there is an appropriate test for nearly everyone: There are test positions suitable for players of all levels covering all phases and most aspects of chess play — and after you take these tests, study the answers, and review your results, *your chess will improve!*

It is at this point that the salesman would say "or you get your money back." No, I won't say this, but I am certain that after you complete any of the tests in this book and review their solutions, *you will be smarter* — that is, you will have more chess conceptual knowledge, and that is what I am interested in. What knowledge is critical for correct play and avoiding mistakes?

In January, 1983 I took a postgraduate academic position at McGill University in Montreal working with Monty Newborn, then Director of the School of Computer Science. The question which we set out to answer was "Are two heads better than one?" This question was addressed from both the computer and human perspectives (See Appendix 1: Experiments in Chess Cognition by Kopec, Newborn and Wu, 1985.) We asked, How will the performance on a chess test set vary when you have two humans collaborating instead of just one working alone? Naturally there are many ways that two humans could interact. What about computers? How would computers perform when more than one processor is used at the same time to play chess? Finally, we addressed the related question, how does performance in chess vary with time? That is, how will the performance of diverse levels of players vary if given 30 seconds, one minute, two minutes, four minutes, eight minutes to solve different test positions? Will stronger players distinguish themselves on the harder eight-minute positions, or on the shorter, easier time-frame positions? The answers to these questions can be found in Appendix 1. The test positions (originally 25) primarily employed for this research were called "The New Positions Test;" they appear after the BK-Test in Chapter 1. A number of other positions used in our test sets are borrowed from the Time Sequence Experiment positions.

Chapter 2 is based on a rather new set of 24 positions called the 1995 Camp Test Positions, devised in the summer of 1995. The idea behind this set of positions is the diversification of some of the concepts tested in Chapter 1.

This test set has had relatively few subjects thus far, and we are eager to gain more data to report on its effectiveness. This test embodies the sum of our experience over many years in testing human and computer subjects. See Appendices 3 and 7 for a summary of Camp Test results from Kopec's Chess Camps.

Since my initial introduction to the discipline of artificial intelligence (AI) while an undergraduate at Dartmouth College in 1973, and computer chess as an AI domain, it has been my research goal to demonstrate how critical domain-specific knowledge is to strong and correct chess play, particularly at the highest levels. Here the term domain-specific knowledge refers to knowledge which is specialized and required for the strong and correct play of the game of chess or any area where specialized knowledge is required for expertise. This special-purpose knowledge may or may not apply to any other intellectual activity. Like other domains where human expertise and excellence have been recognized, such as mathematics and music, chess proficiency does not just suddenly appear. It is based on years of study, learning and praxis.

In 1992 I was a consultant for Saitek International, a leading manufacturer of computer chess programs. It occurred to me that rook and pawn endings, which I estimate may occur as frequently as in one in six games at the master level or above, can be studied from a distinctly knowledge-based perspective. That is the basis of the Rook and Pawn Test of Chapter 3.

In order to round out this book, which had originally been organized to cover the three phases of chess as well as all the chess concepts we could reasonably identify, it was deemed necessary to add another set of test positions. These are contained in Chapter 4: The Other Endings Test. This text covers the major concepts of all major endings.

Over the years it had become clear that the BK-Test and the New Positions Test had proved to be effective in evaluating chess strength for humans and machines in general. However with relative novices rated less than 1500, the test is not so effective in distinguishing how strong these players actually are and what they really know and don't know. That is because players rated around 1500 are not expected to score much more than 5 on the BK-Test. A score of this magnitude cannot be very revealing.

Therefore, before Kopec's Chess Camp in the summer of 1995 it was decided that a new test set should be designed specifically for players who were rated 1500 and less. Hal Terrie developed this test called The Novice Test and it is the basis for Chapter 5. After administering this test to novice subjects at Kopec's Chess Camp in 1995 and to private students, Mr. Terrie has determined that the test is quite valuable for players rated as high as 1700. During the past few years we have also learned that it would be useful to have a test specifically geared for players rated 1600 - 2000 (that is Class B and A respectively). The Bratko-Kopec Test will help identify players between Novice and International Master (quickly) but a test that evaluates the specific intermediate level knowledge deficiencies was also needed. Hence about two years ago Mr. Terrie and I developed The Intermediate Test (Chapter 6).

It has been known for a long time that from a given position humans only search somewhere between fifty and at most two hundred positions (deGroot, 1965) while all successful attempts at programming a computer to play strong chess have involved searching or analyzing thousands, millions, and today, many billions of possible positions. So the ever-present question is: How is it that top humans can play better chess than the top computer chess programs, even though they look at relatively so few positions? The answer is that humans use pattern-recognition to compensate for their deficits in short-term memory and calculational power. It was deGroot, Chase and Simon (1972) and Nievergelt (1977) among others, whose research provided further evidence for this point of view.

Artificial intelligence and cognitive science are concerned with knowledge representation. The focus is how knowledge is acquired, represented, misrepresented, stored, translated, changed and misused. Attempts to measure the value of a chunk of knowledge against more search (in terms of depth and/or breadth, and consequently the number of overall positions considered) naturally follow from research in computer chess. Computer chess program development shifted from decidedly selective search approaches (where depth and breadth of search is sacrificed for knowledge) in the 1970s to brute force implementations (where search is exhaustive to the greatest depth possible in a fixed amount of think time) in the 1980s. The field then reverted to more balanced hybrid methods in the 1990s. Nonetheless, although knowledge and software efficiency remain highly valued, huge multi-million-node searches are still the standard.

Starting with the 17 programs tested and evaluated on the original BK-Test, there has been considerable testing of computer chess programs. For the 1989 6th World Computer Chess Championship in Edmonton, Alberta, Canada, Professor Tony Marsland tested 22 programs on the BK-Test. Then in 1992, while an undergraduate student in computer science at the University of Maine, Shawn Benn tested six commercial programs (Kopec and Benn, 1993). This has been updated with Benn's testing of two more commercial programs, Chessmaster 4000 and Fritz3. (See Appendix 2).

The BK-Test served for many years as a standard for evaluating the strength of computer chess programs. In fact many programs have been trained on the test set as a measure of their suitability and preparation for tournaments. This book has emerged from the understanding that as computer chess programs approach the ultimate goal of the World Championship, we approach a unique era when humans may learn from computer chess programs and vice-versa. In 1990 research I conducted with Berliner and Northam, our real goal was the development of a Taxonomy of Chess Concepts. That has not been fully achieved, and in a sense can never be achieved, at least not from a compilation by humans (by hand). However, this book and its tests do address the essential components of the game of chess (from a knowledge-based point of view).

Many people believe that the six game rematch between IBM's DEEP BLUE program and World Champion Gary Kasparov in May, 1997 which resulted in a narrow 3.5-2.5 victory for the machine, spelled the end of the World Chess Championship for human beings. Certainly the general public emerged from that match with the impression that humans were no longer in control of the World Chess Championship. The public was probably unaware that real human World Championship matches are usually much longer than six games (the standard has been 24 games in most matches sanctioned by FIDE). Even for the educated computer chess follower, the sentiment following Deeper-Blue vs. Kasparov 1997 was that it was just a matter of time before machines will be able to defeat the "Human World Champion" in a match. Certainly in faster time controls the machines have been able to make a significant impression as witnessed by the following recent results:

- A match (May 15-18, 2002) between Junior 7 and GM Mikhail Gurevich (FIDE 2641) was played with a time control of 60 minutes per player. Junior was run on a Pentium 4, 2.0 GHz with 1GB RAM and won 3.5-0.5.

- On May 1, 2002 GM Alexey Dreev (FIDE 2690) played one game at tournament time controls (40/2) vs. Junior 7. The game was a draw.

- In an earlier match (April 13-28, 2002), GM Ilya Smirin (FIDE 2702) played eight games against four programs as presented below from the ChessBase website. Time control was 60 minutes plus a 10 second increment for each player. Smirin won 5-3.

- **Deep Junior** - the reigning Computer World Champion, by Amir Ban and Shay Bushinsky of Israel

- **Deep Shredder 6.02** - reigning single processor World Champion, by Stefin Mayer-Kahlen, Germany, in a new, improved version.

- **Chess Tiger** - top program by Christophe Theron, which has played a sensational 2788 performance in an Argentinian GM tournament.

- **Hiarcs** - new version of the English program best known for its strong positional play, by Mark Uniacke, England.

All programs are the latest and greatest versions, as submitted and supervised by their authors and accompanied with special opening preparation. Hardware: Dual Pentium Intel 1GHz/750 MB RAM (or faster) for the multi processors (Junior, Shredder), P2 2.2 GHz for single processors (Hiarcs, Tiger).

Recent results at slower time controls are varied, but there is a general belief that it is now only a matter of time before the game of chess is conquered by computers ... still how figures like 10^{120} possible positions and 10^{42} reasonable games amongst equal players for 40 moves, are still hard to imagine as being "conquerable," although such prodigious computations may not be necessary to surpass the "human World Chess Champion."

I believe that there will always be a space of the game of chess which humans understand better than the best computer chess program. That space of the game will be decidedly knowledge-based in nature. The kind of knowledge that a 14 ply (seven move) exhaustive search cannot compensate for. I am confident that you will find at least some of the test positions and concepts in this book fitting this prescription. This reinforces the notion that we live in a special time when a genuine symbiosis exists and will continue to evolve: humans can learn from machines and machines can learn from humans.

Chapter 1

The Bratko-Kopec Test

Instructions for taking this test

For each of the following positions, you are allowed a total of two minutes to select your preferred move(s) and to write down up to four choices in order of preference. Write your first choice in the column labeled Preferred Move. Write your secondary choices in the columns labeled 2nd Choice, 3rd Choice, 4th Choice. You will receive partial credit for correct move(s) selections in any column. If your first choice is the correct move, you receive one (1) full point credit, if your second choice is correct it gives ½-point credit, if your third choice is correct it gives ⅓-point credit, and a fourth choice correct gives ¼-point credit.

Answer Sheet for Bratko-Kopec Test

Position Number	Preferred Choice	2nd Choice	3rd Choice	4th Choice	Side to Move
1.	Qd1	b6	Qb6	bc6	Black
2.	f5	h5	bxg4	a5	Black
3.	Ke3	e5	f5	d5	White
4.					White
5.					White
6.					White
7.					White
8.					White
9.					White
10.					Black
11.					White
12.					Black
13.					White
14.					White
15.					White
16.					White
17.					Black
18.					Black
19.					Black
20.					White
21.					White
22.					Black
23.					Black
24.					White

1

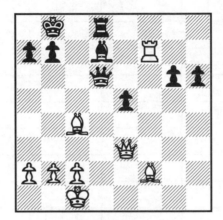

BK Position 1
Black to move

2

BK Position 2
Black to move

3

BK Position 3
White to move

4

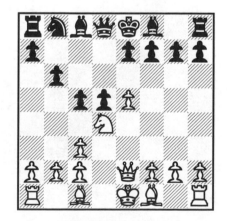

BK Position 4
White to move

5

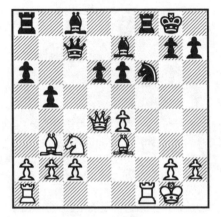

BK Position 5
White to move

6

BK Position 6
White to move

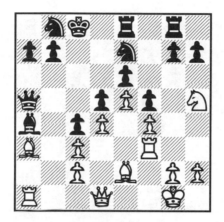

BK Position 7
White to move

8

BK Position 8
White to move

9

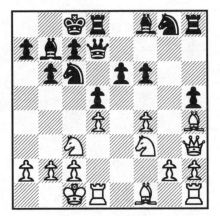

BK Position 9
White to move

10

BK Position 10
Black to move

11

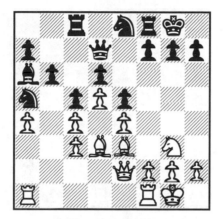

BK Position 11
White to move

12

BK Position 12
Black to move

13

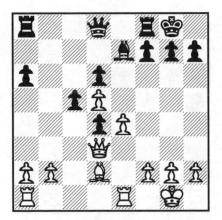

BK Position 13
White to move

14

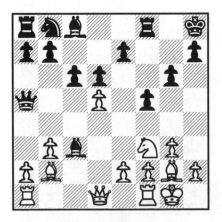

BK Position 14
White to move

15

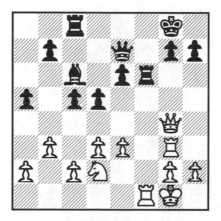

BK Position 15
White to move

16

BK Position 16
White to move

17

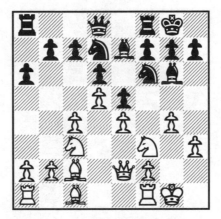

BK Position 17
Black to move

18

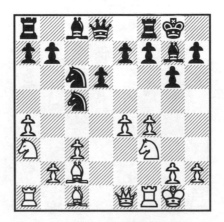

BK Position 18
Black to move

19

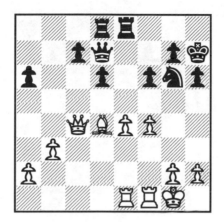

BK Position 19
Black to move

20

BK Position 20
White to move

21

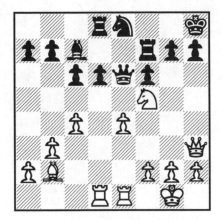

BK Position 21
White to move

22

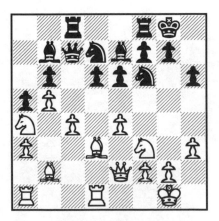

BK Position 22
Black to move

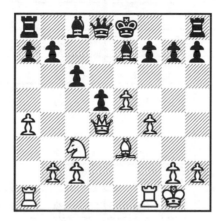

BK Position 23
Black to move

24

BK Position 24
White to move

Solution Key to Bratko-Kopec Test

Position Number	Side to Move	Position Type	Level of Difficulty	Solution
1.	B	Tactical	1	1. ... Qd1 +
2.	B	Lever	2	1. ... f5
3.	W	Lever	3	1. d5
4.	W	Lever	3	1. e6
5.	W	Tactical	3	1. Nd5 (or 1. a4, L)
6.	W	Lever	2	1. g6
7.	W	Tactical	4	1. Nf6
8.	W	Lever	3	1. f5
9.	W	Lever	2	1. f5
10.	B	Tactical	2	1. ... Ne5
11.	W	Lever	2	1. f4
12.	B	Tactical	1	1. ... Bf5
13.	W	Lever	2	1. b4
14.	W	Tactical	2	1. Qe1 or 1. Qd2
15.	W	Tactical	2	1. Qxg7 +
16.	W	Tactical	3	1. Ne4
17.	B	Lever	2	1. ... h5
18.	B	Tactical	4	1. ... Nb3
19.	B	Tactical	3	1. ... Rxe4
20.	W	Lever	2	1. g4
21.	W	Tactical	2	1. Nh6
22.	B	Tactical	4	1. ... Bxe4
23.	B	Lever	4	1. ... f6
24.	W	Lever	2	1. f4

Max = 60

Discussion: The Bratko-Kopec Test

Today there are a number of computer chess programs which play above the master level and a few which can compete on a par with grandmasters. The rudiments of their success are the ability to search exhaustively 11 to 14 ply (half moves) or more. This gives them a superiority over humans of the same rating in solving tactical problems, but not necessarily in positional play. In 1982 Dr. Ivan Bratko and I, then a graduate student at the Machine Intelligence Research Unit at the University of Edinburgh, designed an experiment to try to obtain some quantitative support for the above proposition. Our test positions were chosen with the view that a certain type of positional move (a pawn move called a lever) can play an important role in the strong player's ability to find the best move in a position. Our hypothesis was that strong computer programs will score better than humans of the same rating on tactical problems, but will only find critical positional moves when the best positional move also leads to material gain within the program's search limits.

Since 1982 this test, known as the Bratko-Kopec Test, has been used around the world by computer chess programmers to evaluate the strength of their programs. It has proven a very reliable way to measure the strength of computer chess programs as well as humans. Over the years we have tested about two hundred human subjects (including a former world champion), although results for only about seventy have been published. In addition, many computer programs have used it as a standard against which to measure their progress.

Experimental Design

The Bratko-Kopec Test consists of twenty-four positions (twelve lever and twelve tactical positions). The sources used were primarily Hans Kmoch's 1959 classic *Pawn Power in Chess*, *The Best Move* (Hort and Jansa, 1980), *Informator 18* (Matanovic, 1975), and *Modern Chess Tactics* (Pachman, 1973). In essence, the test requires subjects to find the best move in positions of two fundamentally different types:

(1) tactical positions in which a lack of chess knowledge can be compensated for with calculation; and

(2) lever positions where the lack of chess knowledge cannot be

compensated for. The experiment is portable, is available in electronic form (as are all the test sets and positions discussed in this book) and can be administered, e.g. by mail, (or electronic mail) to any chessplayer, human or machine in the world.

Tactical moves are those which involve the interaction and possible capture of White and Black forces and include:

(1)   checkmate or gain of material; and/or
(2)   a distinct improvement in terms of positional ends (e.g. mobility); and/or
(3)   the defense to some immediate threats.

Our definition of levers is based on Kmoch's but includes a few additions, although the overall concept is unaltered. A lever is a pawn move which:

(1)   offers to trade itself; and
(2)   leads to an ultimate improvement in the pawn structure of the side playing it; and/or
(3)   damages the opponent's pawn structure.

Summary of Results

Our original published results (Kopec and Bratko, 1982) were based on twelve computer programs and thirty-five humans. Readers are referred to this paper for more details about the background of this work, related work and results. Here we will summarize the conclusions of that study:

(1)   The test is a reliable measure of ELO rating both for humans and computer programs. For example, a novice would be expected to score 0-5 (of 24), a club player (rated 1500-1900) should score in the range of 5-10, and expert should score 10-14, a master should score 15-19, a senior master or IM, around 20 or more.
(2)   Computer programs score relatively higher on tactical (T) positions than humans of the same rating.
(3)   Generally, players who score less than fifteen (usually those rated below the master level) have a higher T (tactics) component in their scores than a L (lever) component.
(4)   Primary improvement of players at and above the master level is in the L component.
(5)   Computer programs are lacking in positional knowledge

and therefore score significantly worse in the L positions. This demonstrates the importance of domain-specific knowledge in chess.

Scoring

Scoring on the BK-Test is accomplished by making two columns on the answer sheet (or on a separate sheet of paper), after you have taken the test. Draw a straight line down the length of the sheet with a "T" on the left of the line and an "L" on the right of the line.

As you go down the answer sheet, give the appropriate credit (1, ½, ⅓, ¼, or 0 points) to the appropriate positions in each column. For example, if ... Qd1+ is given as the preferred move in Position 1, then the testee gets a "1" in the T column for Position 1. Then if 1. d5 is suggested as the 3rd Choice move in Position 2, then the testee gets a credit of ⅓ in the L column for Position 2.

Finally, the points in each column are tallied up and the subject gets a Total Score, as well as a T score (for tactics) and an L score (for levers).

You should also add up your level of difficulty score. Give yourself the full level of difficulty number if the correct move was any of your four choices. This is just another way to gain insight into how you (a subject) are performing on a test. You can tell whether you are doing uniformly poorly or well on all kinds of positions, or only on ones which the authors have determined to be particularly easy or difficult.

We believe that there is an increasing gradient of difficulty as you go from the BK Test to the New Positions Test to the Camp Test Positions. Difficulty ratings across these tests are provided with respect to the positions within each test. Positions with a difficulty rating of 4 are deemed hard even for players Master level and above. The difficulty levels in the Novtest (Chapter 5) are, in contrast, with respect to difficulty for players of up to about 1700 playing strength.

Overview and Discussion

A number of human subjects have made interesting comments and criticisms after participating in the experiment. Some suggested that they would have fared much better had they been given an initial few training positions to get some idea of what was being asked for in the experiment. However this would give us no fair method of comparing human results with computer results. Others stated that in a number of positions they could guess the "characteristic" move (often the move scored as correct) in two minutes or under tournament time constraints (usually more than two minutes per move) but that they could not calculate the move's consequences and therefore would probably not play it. Quite a few subjects, particularly those who were students of Bobby Fischer's games, recognized position 15, where Fischer played Qxg7+ against Mecking in the 1970 Palma de Mallorca Interzonal. Nevertheless, we do not feel that either this position or indeed any other that may be recognized, invalidates its inclusion in the experiment. A chessplayer's experience or education can also be used as a contributing factor to help measure his/her ability. Certainly, a few positions in the experiment are not ideal, and a few are even controversial as to what the best move is, but this will not significantly invalidate a human or machine subject's overall score.

There are a number of other possible criticisms of the experiment. First, there is the observation that many programs score surprisingly well, outscoring strong human players who would probably beat these programs under tournament conditions. One explanation for this is that the test conditions were more favorable to machines than to humans. During actual games human players tend to non-uniformly allocate their time to individual moves. Thus a chess master typically spends ten or twenty or more minutes in a position which is identified as "critical" for finding a key move or a key plan, and then might play the next few moves instantly. In contrast, most programs must more or less repeat their whole analysis after each reply by the opponent.

Therefore the programs were probably not as handicapped as humans by the two-minute time limit in the experiment.

There is another explanation for why the experiment ranked some of the programs higher than humans of similar tournament strength. The scores on the test were based on the ability to find a correct move in individual, mutually independent positions, and not on a correct sequence of moves in a whole game. A program may be able to find a correct move(s) in a sequence of positions of the same game. However, although each of the moves may be correct, in a sequence they may not achieve a desired cumulative effect as they may belong to different plans, each of them winning alone but not if combined with others. Therefore, in an actual game, a program's individually correct moves may not be as efficient as a human's sequence of moves. The human's suboptimal sequence of moves may nonetheless consistently follow the same plan. (This idea is Ivan Bratko's.)

Another weakness of the experiment may be that in some of the positions there is more than one good move. Measures of S, L, and T were based on the comparison of one correct move with the move(s) proposed by the subjects, and therefore cannot be considered absolutely reliable. One way to bring this effect into account would be to base the interpretation of the results on the mutual similarity of subjects' responses instead of on the absolute correctness criterion.

References

H. Berliner, D. Kopec and E. Northam, (1990) A Taxonomy of Concepts for Evaluating Chess Strength, *Proceedings of SUPER COMPUTING '90,* New York City, N.Y., Nov. 11-14, pp. 336-43.

H. Berliner, D. Kopec, and E. Northam, (1991). A Taxonomy of Concepts for Evaluating Chess Strength: examples from two difficult categories. In *Advances in Computer Chess 6,* (ed. Don Beal), Ellis Horwood, Chichester, England, pp. 179-91.

V. Hort and V. Jansa (1980) *The Best Move.* RHM Press, New York. (translation, with additions, to original Russian edition of 1976).

H. Kmoch, (1959) *Pawn Power in Chess.* David McKay, New York.

D. Kopec and I. Bratko, (1982) The Bratko-Kopec Experiment: a comparison of human and computer performance in chess. In *Advances in Computer Chess 3* (ed. M.R.B. Clarke), Pergamon Press, Oxford, pp. 57-72.

D. Kopec, M. Newborn and W. Yu (1986). Experiments in Chess Cognition. In *Advances in Computer Chess 4* (ed. D. Beal) Pergamon Press, Oxford, England, pp. 59-79.

D. Kopec, (1990) Advances in Man-Machine Play, in *Computers, Chess and Cognition,* eds. T.A. Marsland and J. Schaeffer, Springer-Verlag, New York, pp. 9-33.

D. Kopec, and W. Benn, (1992) Comparison and Testing of Six Commercial Computer Chess Programs. *Proceedings of Workshop on Computer Chess at the World Microcomputer Chess Championship,* Madrid, Spain.

L. Pachman (1973) *Modern Chess Tactics.* Routledge & Kegan Paul, London. (Translated by P.H. Clarke from original Czech version of 1970.)

T. A. Marsland (1990). The Bratko-Kopec Test Revisited. In *Computers, Chess and Cognition.* Eds. T.A. Marsland and J. Schaeffer, Springer-Verlag, New York, pp. 217-223. (See Appendix 1-C this edition, pp. 260-270)

A. Matanovic, (1975) *Informant* No. 18. Belgrade.

D. Kopec and H. Terrie (1997) *Test, Evaluate, and Improve Your Chess;* a knowledge-based approach, Hypermodern Press, San Francisco, (1st Edition) 235 pp.

CAMP KOPEC

The New Positions Test

Instructions for taking this test

This test should be taken in the exact same way as the previous, Bratko-Kopec Test. For each of the following positions, you are allowed a total of two minutes to select your preferred move(s) and to write down up to four choices in order of preference. Write your first choice in the column labeled Preferred Move. Write your secondary choices in the columns labeled 2nd Choice, 3rd Choice, 4th Choice. You will receive partial credit for correct move(s) selections in any column. If your first choice is the correct move, you receive one (1) full point credit, if your second choice is correct it gives $\frac{1}{2}$-point credit, if your third choice is correct it gives $\frac{1}{3}$-point credit, and a fourth choice correct gives $\frac{1}{4}$-point credit.

Answer Sheet for New Positions Test

Position Number	Preferred Choice	2nd Choice	3rd Choice	4th Choice	Side to Move
1.					Black
2.					White
3.					Black
4.					White
5.					White
6.					Black
7.					Black
8.					White
9.					White
10.					Black
11.					White
12.					White
13.					Black
14.					Black
15.					White
16.					White
17.					White
18.					White
19.					White
20.					White
21.					White
22.					Black
23.					Black
24.					White

25

NewPos Position 1
Black to move

26

NewPos Position 2
White to move

27

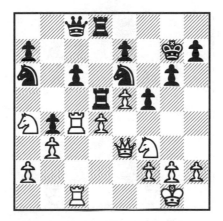

NewPos Position 3
Black to move

28

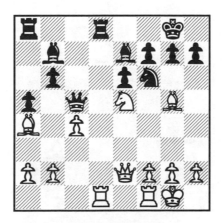

NewPos Position 4
White to move

29

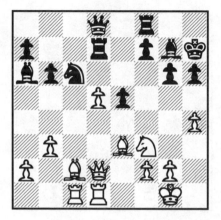

NewPos Position 5
White to move

30

NewPos Position 6
Black to move

31

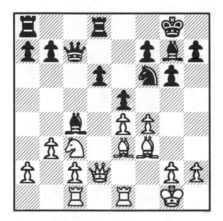

NewPos Position 7
Black to move

32

NewPos Position 8
White to move

33

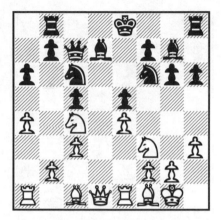

NewPos Position 9
White to move

34

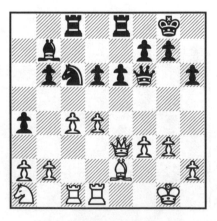

NewPos Position 10
Black to move

35

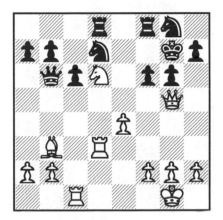

NewPos Position 11
White to move

36

NewPos Position 12
White to move

37

NewPos Position 13
Black to move

38

NewPos Position 14
Black to move

39

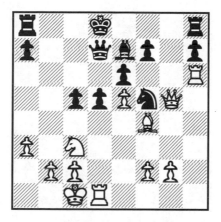

NewPos Position 15
White to move

40

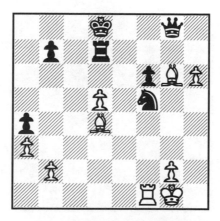

NewPos Position 16
White to move

41

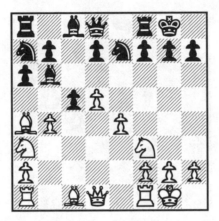

NewPos Position 17
White to move

42

NewPos Position 18
White to move

43

NewPos Position 19
White to move

44

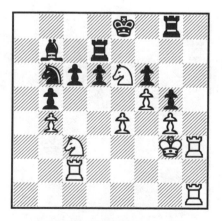

NewPos Position 20
White to move

45

NewPos Position 21
White to move

46

NewPos Position 22
Black to move

47

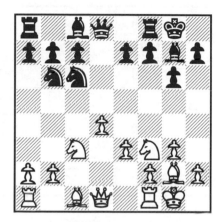

NewPos Position 23
Black to move

48

NewPos Position 24
White to move

Solution Key for New Positions Test

Position Number	Side to Move	Position Type	Level of Difficulty	Solution
1.	B	Lever	2	1. ... b5
2.	W	Tactical	3	1. Kh3
3.	B	Lever	2	1. ... c5
4.	W	Tactical	3	1. Bxf6
5.	W	Lever	2	1. h5
6.	B	Tactical	4	1. ... Nxf3 +
7.	B	Lever	4	1. ... d5
8.	W	Tactical	3	1. Na1
9.	W	Lever	3	1. b4
10.	B	Lever	3	1. ... d5
11.	W	Tactical	3	1. Nf5 +
12.	W	Tactical	2	1. e6
13.	B	Tactical	4	1. ... b4
14.	B	Lever	3	1. ... e5
15.	W	Tactical	4	1. Qxf5 or 1. Rf6
16.	W	Tactical	4	1. Bb6 +
17.	W	Lever	2	1. d6
18.	W	Lever	2	1. Be3 or 1. b4
19.	W	Tactical	3	1. Qe3
20.	W	Lever	2	1. e5
21.	W	Tactical	3	1. h7
22.	B	Tactical	3	1. ... Kg4
23.	B	Lever	2	1. ... e5
24.	W	Tactical	3	1. Kg2

Max = 69

Discussion: The New Positions Test

The test you have just taken measured the same knowledge as in the previous test: your knowledge of levers, the concept introduced in the first test set. If you have learned this concept well as a result of the first test's material, then this knowledge will be demonstrated in your performance on this second test set. We believe that you will find these positions more diverse in the types of tactical and lever motifs that are presented.

In general, this set is probably a little harder than the Bratko-Kopec Test because the motifs, both in terms of levers and tactics, are more subtle. The positions are not as characteristic or typical of the levers and tactics represented.

Examples of some of the concepts tested include: lever timing, unique king moves, forcing variations, sweeper-sealer levers, trapped pieces with miniature combinations, characteristic levers, logical defense, finding the best order of implementation, and queen sacrifices for various purposes and forms of compensation.

Scoring

Scoring on the New Positions Test is done in exactly the same way as on the Bratko-Kopec Test of Chapter 1. Again, this is accomplished by making two columns on the answer sheet or another sheet of paper (after you have taken the test), Using a straight line down the length of the sheet with a"T" on the left of the line and an "L" on the right of the line.

As you go down the answer sheet, give the appropriate credit (1, $\frac{1}{2}$, $\frac{1}{3}$, $\frac{1}{4}$, or 0 points) to the appropriate positions in each column. Finally, the points in each column are tallied up and the subject gets a Total Score, as well as a T score for tactics and an L score for levers. Once again, you should also add up your level of difficulty score, e.g.

Position Number	Side to Move	Preferred Move	2nd Choice	3rd Choice	4th Choice	T	L
1	B	... b5					1
2	W	Kg3	Kh3			1/2	
3	B	... c5					1

Complete Solutions to Bratko-Kopec Test

1

BK Position 1 (T)
Andersson-Knuttson
Sweden, 1974
Chess Informant 18
(Combination #9)
Black to move

1. ... Qd1+ 2. Kxd1 Bg4+ 3. Ke1 Rd1#. This requires little explanation. If you have seen this theme of a queen sacrifice followed by a double discovered check then you will find it.

2

BK Position 2 (L)
Evans-Rossolimo
U.S. Open, 1955
Pawn Power in Chess
(Diagram 164)
Black to move

1. ... f5. This exemplifies a classic lever around which Black has organized nearly all his forces. Without knowing about levers, computer programs can still select this move because it improves mobility, gains space and attacks the center. This position is also an example of the value of chess erudition. Those with a strong chess historical background would know that such positions can arise from the closed variations of the Ruy Lopez when White plays d5. In such instances the structure becomes that of a King's Indian Defense.

3

1. d5 cxd5 2. e5 R6d7
(2. ... d4? 3. exd6 dxc3
4. dxe7+ wins a piece.)
3. Nd4 This is an example of a very characteristic lever, the
"sweeper sealer twist"
(Kmoch, 1959).
It involves a long-term

BK Position 3 (L)
Bogoljubow-Spielmann
Match Game, 1932
Pawn Power in Chess
(Diagram 144)
White to move

pawn sacrifice where, at the end of the principal variation (above),
White has: (1) gained full control of the open c-file, (2) sealed off
Black's half-open d-file, (3) gained a tremendous central post for
his knight, (4) weakened Black's pawns into three groups (three
islands), and (5) gained a kingside majority of pawns. Bogoljubow
found 1. d5! but later erred to only draw.

4

1. e6 fxe6 (1. ... cxd4 2.
Qb5+ Nd7 [2. ... *Bd7 3.*
Qxd5 or 3. exf7+ also
wins] 3. Qxd5+-) **2.**
Qh5+ Kd7 (2. ... g6 3.
Qe5± Rg8 4. Nxe6
White is winning.) **3.**
Nf3. This is an example of the "Night at-

BK Position 4 (L)
Spielmann-Walter
Trenstschin-Teplitz,
1928
Pawn Power in Chess
(Diagram 146)
White to move

tack" (another Kmoch term). The idea of this pawn lever is to split
Black's game into two halves caused by his doubled e-pawns. This
makes Black's coordination of forces and development difficult. In
such instances, it is important for White to control and blockade
Black's doubled pawns with pieces. It is arguable that 1. e6 is a
very tactical move, but the game continuation (main variation
above) indicates a pawn sacrifice for positional as well as tactical
ends, despite the fact that White delivered mate on move 20!

5

BK Position 5 (T)
Rogolewicz-Jarecz
Poland, 1974
Chess Informant 18
(Combination #24)
White to move

1. Nd5! is a typical Sicilian tactical stroke which exploits Black's hanging rook on a8. The variations below cover only a few of the many complicated possibilities after the move 1. Nd5. The lever 1. a4! was found by 12-year-old Mark Condie (now an IM) and is also an acceptable first move for which White gets full credit under L. **1. ... Nxd5** (*1. ... Qb7 2. Nb6 Rb8 3. Nxc8 Qxc8 4. e5+-*) **2. Bxd5** the game continuation. Because of a possible defense, missed by Black in the game, an attempt to improve is 2. ... Ref8+ Kxf8 (*2. ... Bxf8 3. Bxd5 Rb8 4. Qa7 transposes to the game*) and now:

(a) 3. exd5 e5 4. Rf1+ Bf6 (*4. ... Kg8 5. Qxe5! dxe5 6. d6+ Qc4 7. Bxc4+ bxc4 8. dxe7*) 5. Qe4 Kg8 6. c3 intending Bc2, with complicated play when the outcome is not clear;

(b) 3. Bxd5 3. ... exd5 4. Rf1+ Ke8 (*4. ... Kg8 5. Qxd5++-; 4. ... Bf6 5. e5!! dxe5 6. Qxd5 and now the position becomes very unclear. The only move is 6. ... Qb7, found by Fritz3. White can make life miserable for the Black king but a forced win is not evident. (The student is encouraged to analyze the position further on his own.)* 5. Qxd5 Another unclear position where White has some pressure but nothing forced.

2. ... Rb8? Better was 2. ... Rxf1+ 3. Rxf1 Rb8 4. Qa7 Bd8! This saving defensive move was also found by Mark Condie, and is the reason for the attempt to improve White's play with 2. Rxf8+. The game concluded: **3. Rxf8+ Bxf8 4. Qa7 Qxa7 5. Bxa7 exd5 6. Bxb8 1-0.**

6

1. g6. This temporary endgame pawn sacrifice is necessary immediately, in view of Black's threat to equalize with ... g6 and ... Kf8-e8. White will follow with Kg4-g5 etc., winning easily. **1. ...**

BK Position 6 (L)
Composition, Kmoch
Pawn Power in Chess
(Diagram 105)
White to move

fxg6 2. Kg4 Kh7 3. Kg5! It is important that White does not allow himself to be diverted. He should (1) keep control of the d-file and prevent Black's rook from becoming active; (2) advance his king as far as possible; (3) advance his queenside pawns until Black is forced into *zugzwang* (out of moves without loss of material). 3. Re7? chasing the e-pawn, would be bad because of 3. ... Kg8 4. Rxe6?? Kf7 wins for Black.

7

This is one of the harder positions where many humans miss the main tactical theme:

BK Position 7 (T)
Golyak-Gaiduk
Modern Chess Tactics
(Diagram 3)
White to move

1. Nf6! gxf6 2. exf6 and White either forks the rooks or wins the knight on e7. Many subjects suggest 1. Bb4, a good intermediary move, but there is no way of determining whether 2. Nf6 is their intended follow-up.

8

BK Position 8 (L)
Alekhine-Yates
Hastings, 1926
Pawn Power in Chess
(Diagram 65)
White to move

Black suffers from a classic weakness of the dark squares, hence:

1. f5 eventually forces access to the f4-square for White's knight. **1. ... g5.** Fine discusses in *Basic Chess Endings* (#256, page 247) that after 1. ...gxf5 2. Nf4 Bc6 3. Nxh5 Kf8 he couldn't find a win for White. However, I (DK) believe that we have found a straightforward winning plan for White as follows: 1) Play Nf4 and then e6 combined with h4 2) Get the N to c3 via f4, e2. 3) Get the White King to f4. 4) After advancing the a-pawn as far as possible use the h-pawn as a decoy. 5) Win the a-pawn. White's a-pawn wins the game. **2. h4 f6 3. hxg5 fxg5 4. Ng1!! Bd7** (4. ... h4 5. g4! Ba4 6. Ke2! c3 7. Nh3 c2 8. Kd2. Notice that Black's passed c-pawn is ineffective because of his inability to control the dark squares. 8. ... Bb5 9. Nxg5 Be2 10. f6+ Ke8 11. e6 Bxg4 12. f7+ Ke7 13. Nh7 and wins.) **5. f6+ Ke8 6. Nf3 g4 7. Nh4 Be6 8. Ng6 Bf7 9. Nf4 Kd7 10. Ke2 a5 11. Ke3.** Black has no useful moves and will soon have to move king or bishop.

9

BK Position 9 (L)
Jansa - R. Weinstein
Helsinki, 1961
The Best Move
(Diagram #14)
White to move

1. f5. Many subjects choose 1. Bb5 but the main theme is to follow the lever 1. f5 with 2. Bd3 and then Ne2-f4 etc. White implements the famous Nimzowitsch strategy: blockade, attack, destroy. Black cannot play 1. ... e5 because after 2. dxe5 his pawn is pinned.

10

1. ... Ne5 Removes the blockader and leads to the opening of the g1-a7 diagonal. (1. ... Qc5, suggested by many computer programs, is interesting but clearly not best. White has 2. c4 or 2. c3 as possible

BK Position 10 (T)
Kabadzjan-Cibelasvili
USSR, 1974

Chess Informant 18
(Combination #45)
Black to move

answers.) **2. Rxd4** (2. Rd1 Neg4!) **2. ... Neg4!! 3. fxg4 Nxg4** Black wins material. For example, **4. Qf3 Rxe2 5. Qxe2 Qxd4+.**

11

1. f4 is a straightforward space-gaining lever, though if Black's pieces (especially his knights) had easy access to e5 then this would be a poor move due to the resulting backwardness of White's e-pawn.

BK Position 11 (L)
R. Byrne-Kotov
USA-USSR Team
Match, 1954

Pawn Power in Chess
(Diagram 177)
White to move

12

BK Position 12 (T)
Composition, 1973
Modern Chess Tactics
(Diagram 3)
Black to move

1. ... Bf5. A simple defensive tactic, the only move which defends both of White's threats. This is a type of control position which everyone is expected to solve.

13

BK Position 13 (L)
Pfeiffer-Trifunovich
West Germany-
Yugoslavia
Team Match, 1954
Pawn Power in Chess
(Diagram 69)
White to move

Black suffers from a weakness of the light squares, which Kmoch called "leucopenia." The sophisticated lever **1. b4** enables White to advance his central pawns after bxc5 and Qc4. If Black plays 1. ... cxb4 2. Bxb4 one of his weak doubled d-pawns will soon fall. No credit for 1. f4, since White does not threaten e5 and Black has ... a5 with counterplay on the b-file.

14

1. Qd2 A straightforward crossfire/pinning tactic that wins material. 1. Qe1 would also work.

BK Position 14 (T)
Robatsch-Jansa
Soci, 1974
Chess Informant 18
(Combination #32)
White to move

15

1. Qxg7+ Qxg7 2. Rxf6. After the further **2. ... Qxg3 3. hxg3**, later followed by **g4-g5-g6**, Fischer managed to trade off his extra, doubled g-pawn to remain a pawn ahead. (Overloaded Black Queen.)

BK Position 15 (T)
Fischer-Mecking
Palma de Mallorca
Interzonal, 1970
White to move

16

BK Position 16 (T)
Vasilchuk-Bobolovitch
1973
Modern Chess Tactics
(Diagram 18)
White to move

This is a tactical position where after:

1. Ne4 White is guaranteed at least positional gains with Nd6+ to follow. Thus: **1. ... Be6** (1. ... dxe4 2. Bxf7+ Kxf7 3. Qxd8 hxg5 and although Black has obtained three pieces for the queen, his exposed king, pawn deficit, and poor piece coordination mean that he does not have sufficient compensation.) **2. Nd6+** with a big positional plus. **2. ... Kd7 3. Bh4** with f4 to follow. (Pins, overload, and forks.)

17

BK Position 17 (L)
Van Den Bosch-Kmoch
Baarn, 1941
Pawn Power in Chess
(Diagram 176)
Black to move

1. ... h5 The idea is ... hxg4, followed by ... Nh7-g5. If 2. g5 Nh7 3. h4 f6! The move 1. ... Ne8 was played in a game Alekhine-Johner, with Black getting a cramped and miserable game. 1. ... h5! was an improvement played by Kmoch in one of his games. The idea is that White has weakened himself on the dark squares ("melanpenia") and this is the way to exploit them.

18

This is from a Fischer game which exemplifies that achievement of the two bishops against bishop and knight in a semi-open position is, at the highest levels of play, tantamount to material

BK Position 18 (T)
Maric-Fischer
Skopje, 1967
Black to move

gain. After: **1. ... Nb3! 2. Bxb3 Qb6+ 3. Kh1 Qxb3** White relinquishes the two bishop advantage to Black and is left weakened on the light squares. Very few humans found 1. ... Nb3, most stronger ones suggesting 1. ... Qb6, 1. ... Be6 or even 1. ... d5. Although interesting, none of these is as clear as 1. ... Nb3. (Double attack, check fork.)

19

1. ... Rxe4! The fork trick in action. After: **2. Rxe4 d5 3. Qxa6 dxe4 4. Be3 Qg4!** Keres quickly translates his central advantage into a winning kingside attack. **5. Qc4 Rd3! 6. Bc1** (6. Qxe4?? Qe2-+) **6. ... Nh4! 7. Qxe4+** (7. g3 Rxg3+-+; 7. Rf2 Rd1+-+; 7. Qc2 f5! with

BK Position 19 (T)
Euwe-Keres
World Championship Tournament,
The Hague, 1948
Pawn Power in Chess
(Diagram 154)
Black to move

the deadly threat of ... e3 [Kmoch]). **7. ... f5 8. Qb7 c6 9. Qxc6 Rc3 10. Qd5 Rc5! 11. Qd2 Rxc1!** The point being 12. Rxc1 Nf3+. Black won. (Fork trick.)

20

BK Position 20 (L)
Euwe-Flohr
10th Match Game,
Karlsbad, 1932
Pawn Power in Chess
(Diagram 90)
White to move

1. g4 This might be called an attacking lever, since the purpose is purely to expose the pawn shield in front of the Black king. After **1. ... fxg4 2. Qxg4 Rg7 3. Qh5,** White will follow with f5. Notice how inactive Black's bishops are.

21

BK Position 21 (T)
Tarrasch-Blackburne
Manchester, 1890
Modern Chess Tactics
(Diagram 27)
White to move

1. Nh6 wins the exchange in all variations. You can't afford to miss such opportunities. (Discovery, double attack.)

22

This is the hardest position of the entire set, at least for humans. Perhaps the fact that only one human subject of the original thirty-five (IM Craig Prichett) and only three of the seventeen computer programs in the original test, found the best move, is highly significant.

BK Position 22 (T)
Najdorf-Reshevsky
Match, New York, 1952
Modern Chess Tactics
(Diagram 50)
Black to move

Humans suggest reasonable and/or interesting moves such as 1. ... Rfd8, Nc5, d5, Ne5 and Nh5 which often come into consideration in similar positions. However, only the un-usual combination beginning with:

1. ... Bxe4 2. Bxe4 followed by **2. ... Qxc4** leads to immediate advantage. **3. Qxc4 Rxc4 4. Nxb6 Rxe4 5. Nxd7 Nxd7.** Depth of search seems not to be the problem for humans in trying to find this combination; rather more likely is its individuality and the fact that many other good moves seem possible. (Decoy with double attack.)

23

BK Position 23 (L)
Jansa-Kavalek
Harrochev, 1963
The Best Move
(Diagram 24)
Black to move

This is also a hard position in the sense that the "normal" 1. ... Bf5 is confronted with the very interesting 2. g4!?, which most people (and computers) fail to consider adequately. Then, on either 2. ... Bxg4 or 2. ... Bxc2 White plays 3. f5 threatening f6. The move:

1. ... f6 is an essential head pawn lever which meets the threat of 2. f5. After **2. exf6 Bxf6 3. Qc5** Black has a number of choices, including 3. ... Be7, 3. ... Qe7 and 3. ... Kf7. Instead, in the game Kavalek played 1. ... f5? when after 2. a5!, followed by b4, Na4, Qc3 and Bc5, trading Black's good bishop, he found himself in a horrible bind.

24

BK Position 24 (L)
Szabo-Ivkov
Buenos Aires, 1955
Pawn Power in Chess
(Diagram 160)
White to move

1. f4 The indicated duo lever, since White's superior pieces make it easier for him to maintain tension in the center. If now, **1. ... g5!?** as played **2. g3!** (not 2. fxg5?! f4 3. gxh6 Bxh6 etc., with space and play for a pawn) with White keeping an advantage, since exchanges on e4 or f4 will only improve White's pieces.

Complete Solutions to the New Positions Test

25

Black has the duo-forming lever type expansion ... b5, and should not delay it as occurred in actual play with 1. ... 0-0?, when 2. a4 made ... b5 nearly impossible for the rest of the game. After **1. ... b5,** Black need not fear the pin 2. Qe2 since he has adequate resources with 2. ... Nxd5.

NewPos Position 1 (L)
W. Watson-Kopec
Phillips & Drew, 1982
Black to move

26

1. Kh3 (This is based on a study by Botvinnik. Note that the solution in *Basic Chess Endings* is wrong.) All other moves allow Black to queen as well. **1. ... Ke5** (1. ... f4 2. h6 f3 3. h7 f2 4. Kg2+-) **2. Kg3 Ke6 3. Kf4 Kf6 4. h6 Kg6 5. h7 Kxh7 6. Kxf5+-.**

NewPos Position 2 (T)
Kmoch-Van Scheltinga
Amsterdam, 1936
Basic Chess Endings
(#55)
White to move

27

NewPos Position 3 (L)
Furman-Ribli
Vidmar Memorial, 1975
World Chess Title Contenders and Their Styles
Kopec/Pritchett, 2002
Black to move

The lever **1. ... c5!** which (1) gets rid of Black's backward c-pawn; (2) seals off the hole on c5 from White's pieces; and (3) opens the d-file for Black's doubled rooks, is called for here.

28

NewPos Position 4 (T)
Kleboe-Weeden
Glasgow, 1981
Mastering Chess, p. 38
White to move

1. Bxf6 Bxf6 2. Nd7 Qc7 This would be best. (2. ... Qg5 3. f4 Qg6 4. Bc2 Qh6 5. Nxb6 Bd4+ 6. Rxd4 Rxd4 7. Nxa8; 2. ... Qb4 3. b3 with the idea of Qe3.) **3. b3 Bc6 4. Bxc6 Qxc6 5. Nxf6+ gxf6** doesn't give White much. The point of this example is that White can force play and Black must play very accurately to maintain the balance.

29

1. h5 (1. dxc6 Rxd2 2. Rxd2 Qa8 3. Rd6 deserves consideration) **1. ... Ne7 2. Nh4! Rxd5 3. hxg6+ fxg6 4. Qxd5!!** (4. Bxg6+?! Nxg6 5. Qxd5 Qxh4; 4. Nxg6? Rxd2 5. Nxf8+ Kg8) **4. ... Nxd5 5. Nxg6 Bb7** (5. ... Qa8 was perhaps the best try.) **6. Nxf8+**

NewPos Position 5 (L)
Kopec-Ocipoff
Pan Am
Intercollegiate,
1974
Mastering Chess, p. 106
White to move

Kg8 7. Ne6 Qf6 8. Nxg7 Kxg7 9. Be4 Qf7 (9. ... Nxe3 10. Rd7+ Kg8 11. Rxb7+-) **10. Bxd5 Bxd5 11. Rc3** Black has no answer to this rook doubling maneuver. **11. ... Qb7 12. Rdc1 Qa6 13. Rc7+ Kg6 14. Rd7 Qd3 15. Rd6+ Kf5 16. Rxh6 a5 17. Rc8 Qb1+ 18. Kh2 Qxa2 19. Rxb6 Qe2 20. Rh8 Qf1 21. f3 e4 22. g4+** 22. Rh5 is mate but both sides were in time trouble. **22. ... Ke5 23. Rh5#.** (Attacking lever.)

30

Black notices that both knights are effectively trapped but his can *desperado* itself effectively with a small combination:

1. ... Nxf3+!! 2. gxf3 (2. Qxf3? Qxb5) **2. ... Qg5!** A quiet move with a sting. **3. Nxg6+ hxg6** Black is better due to the split pawns on White's kingside.

NewPos Position 6 (T)
McKay-Kopec
Scottish
Championship, 1981
Mastering Chess, p. 47
Black to move

31

NewPos Position 7 (L)
Rauzer-Botvinnik
USSR 1933
Meet the Masters, p. 147
Black to move

A famous early Dragon Variation Botvinnik game where he favorably burst open the center with the strongest "Sicilian Lever":

1. ... d5!

(a) 2. bxc4 dxe4 recovers the piece with the better game;
(b) 2. Nxd5 Bxd5 3. exd5 e4 4. Be2 Nxd5;
(c) 2. fxe5 Nxe4 3. Bxe4 dxe4 followed by... Qxe5
    with advantage.
(d) 2. exd5 e4! 3. bxc4 exf3 with a strong attack.

32

NewPos Position 8 (T)
Jansa-Bilek
Polanica Zdroj, 1968
The Best Move,
(Diagram #75)
White to move

This is a unique case where it's best to defend fully and properly for one more move and then consummate the attack. Therefore:

1. Na1 (a very unusual retreat) and then the straightforward threat of Qh2, hxg6, Qh7+ and Bh6 is too strong. After 1. Nd4?!, Black has defensive resources starting with 1. ... Bxd4.

33

Here there are a number of attacking concepts including 1. Nd6+(?), 1. Qd6 (also not best), and the positional 1. a5, but:

1. b4 is clearly sharpest, with many threats, e.g. **1. ... cxb4 2. cxb4 Nxb4 3. Ba3** etc. An example of an attacking lever and a pawn sacrifice.

NewPos Position 9 (L)
Andersson-Portisch
Skopje, 1972
World Chess Title Contenders and Their Styles, p. 100
White to move

34

1. ... d5 The lever 1. ... d5 has a paradoxical effect in that it forces open the position for Black's pieces while appearing to shut in the queen's bishop, e.g. 2. cxd5 exd5 3. Q-any Nxd4 or 2. c5 bxc5 3. Rxc5 Nxd4 again. On 1. ... e5 2. d5.

NewPos Position 10 (L)
Yusatake-Kopec
New England Open, 1983
Black to move

35

NewPos Position 11 (T)
Alekhine-Lasker
Zurich, 1934
Meet the Masters, p. 31
White to move

Alekhine finished this famous attacking game against Lasker with a combination capped by a queen sacrifice, leading to mate:
   1. Nf5+ Kh8 2. Qxg6!
Black resigned, since if 2. ... hxg6 3. Rh3 mate.

36

NewPos Position 12 (L)
Spassky-Fischer
13th Match Game, 1972
World Chess Title Contenders and their Styles
(Analysis p. 55)
White to move

1. e6 It is easy to see that the attacking lever 1. e6 splits Black's position in half while shutting his queen out of the game. However, the Black king's bishop is suddenly very active. Still, 1. e6!? is White's best chance to seek active counterplay for a pawn. Smyslov gives the further continuation 1. ... Nc4 2. Qe2 (2. Qb4 is another idea) 2. ... Nxb2 3. Nf5 as unclear.

37

The continuation here is from what has been deemed the "greatest game of all time." Alekhine continued: **1. ... b4!! 2. Rxa8 bxc3 3. Rxe8 c2 4. Rxf8+ Kh7** and the new Black queen was decisive.

NewPos Position 13 (T)
Bogoljubow-Alekhine
Hastings, 1922
Meet the Masters,
p. 40
Black to move

38

Black has the "duo busting" lever: **1. ... e5!** which virtually forces **2. fxe5** when after **2. ... Be6** he was better despite being two pawns down.

NewPos Position 14 (L)
Kaplan-Kopec
Continental Open, 1975
Black to move

39

NewPos Position 15 (T)
Kopec-Wagner
Seven-board blindfold exhibition, University of Illinois, 1979
White to move

White was very pleased to find the combination:

1. Qxf5!! exf5 2. Rxd5 leaving Black with five shattered pawns in the endgame (especially as this was one of seven games played by White in a blindfold exhibition). 1. Rf6 was also possible since 1. ... Bxf6 2. Qxf6+ Kc7 3. Nxd5+ is very strong.

40

NewPos Position 16 (T)
Kopec-McNab
Edinburgh Congress, 1981
Mastering Chess, p. 105
White to move

White has been down a queen for two bishops and two pawns for some moves, as he can remain with 1. Bxf5. However:

1. Bb6+! virtually forced the interfering **1. ... Ke7** followed by **2. h7** ("intermezzo") which in turn forced **2. ... Qg7**

3. Re1+ Kd6 4. Bxf5 Re7. Now White realized that after the exchange of rooks, the two bishops and two pawns would overpower the Black king and queen. Thus: **5. Rxe7 Kxe7 6. Bc5+ Kf7 7. d6** and White soon won. (Check with interference.)

41

The ram lever action:

1. d6 disrupts communications between Black's two flanks, stymying the development of his queen's bishop and queen's rook.

NewPos Position 17 (L)
Fuderer-Tartakower
Bled, 1950
Pawn Power in Chess
(Diagram #149)
White to move

42

White should not play 1. f4?, leaving the e5 square as a beautiful "hole" for Black's pieces after 1. ... exf4. Instead White should play:

1. Be3 or **1. b4,** supporting the lever c5.

NewPos Position 18 (L)
Tartakower-Lasker
New York, 1924
Pawn Power in Chess
(Diagram #175)
White to move

43

NewPos Position 19 (T)
Alekhine-Wolfe
Bad Pistyan, 1922
Meet the Masters, p. 22
White to move

This was a remarkable exception to the general rule where three White queen moves in the first nine moves were the best way to confound the development of Black's pieces. **1. Qe3 g6 2. Nf3 Qc7 3. Qc3 Rg8 4. Be3 b6 5. Nbd2 Bg7 6. Bd4 Bxd4 7. Qxd4 Bb5 8. Bxb5+ axb5 9. 0-0** and White went on to win.

44

NewPos Position 20 (L)
Lasker-Capablanca
St. Petersburg, 1914
Pawn Power in Chess
(Diagram #140)
White to move

1. e5! A classic "sweeper sealer twist." On 1. ... dxe5 or ... fxe5, the move Ne4 follows decisively.

45

1. h7! This is much better than the immediate 1. Qd4?!, as played (threatening 2. Qxb6+), when Black has 1. ... Qxd6 (forced) 2. exd6 Bg6 with some defensive resources. **1. ... Rh8 2. Qd4 Qxd6 3. exd6 Rxh7 4. Qe4** and White wins. (Forcing sequence with correct order.)

NewPos Position 21 (T)
Kopec-McKay
Scottish Ch. Playoff,
Game 1, 1981
Mastering Chess, p. 42
White to move

46

1. ... Kg4 (1. ... Kf4? 2. Rh4+ Kg3 3. Rh7 Kf4 4. e6) **2. Rh7 Ra6+ 3. Kxf7 Ra7+ 4. Kg6 Rxh7 5. Kxh7 Kf5,** clearly drawing. The king must approach with caution.

NewPos Position 22 (T)
Hort-Wade
Hastings, 1972
The Best Move
(Diagram #170)
Black to move

47

NewPos Position 23 (L)
Sapi-Ribli
Hungary, 1974
Best Games of the Young Grandmasters, p. 147
Black to move

Black has a number of moves which may possibly lead to equality. Most direct is the lever:

1. ... e5 so that on **2. d5 Ne7 3. e4** and later **... c6** etc.

48

NewPos Position 24 (T)
Hort-Ribli
Budapest, 1973
The Best Move, No. 96
White to move

White should not be too greedy and fall into 1. Rxb6? Rh3+ 2. Kf2 Rxe3! Thus best is the "intermezzo":

1. Kg2 first, and after **1. ... Re1 2. Kf2** and only then **3. Rxb6.**

Chapter Two

The Camp Test 1995

Instructions for taking this test

This test should be taken in the exact same way as the previous, Bratko-Kopec and New Position tests. You are allowed a total of two minutes for each of the following positions to select your preferred move(s) and to write down up to four choices in order of preference. Write your first choice in the column labeled "Preferred Move". Write your secondary choices in the columns labeled "2nd Choice," "3rd Choice," "4th Choice." You will receive partial credit for correct move(s) selections in any column. If your first choice is the correct move, you receive one (1) full point; if your second choice is correct, 1/2-point credit; if your third choice is correct it gives 1/3-point credit, and a fourth choice correct gives 1/4-point credit.

Answer Sheet for Camp Test 1995

Position Number	Preferred Choice	2nd Choice	3rd Choice	4th Choice	Side to Move
1.					Black
2.					White
3.					Black
4.					White
5.					White
6.					White
7.					Black
8.					White
9.					White
10.					Black
11.					White
12.					Black
13.					White
14.					White
15.					White
16.					Black
17.					Black
18.					White
19.					Black
20.					White
21.					White
22.					Black
23.					Black
24.					White

49

Camp Test Position 1
Black to move

50

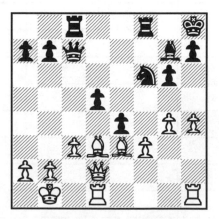

Camp Test Position 2
White to move

51

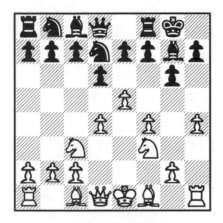

Camp Test Position 3
Black to move

52

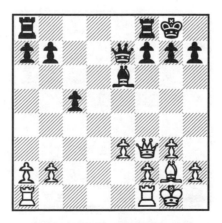

Camp Test Position 4
White to move

53

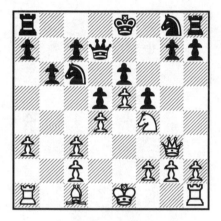

Camp Test Position 5
White to move

54

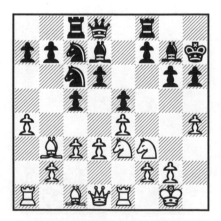

Camp Test Position 6
White to move

55

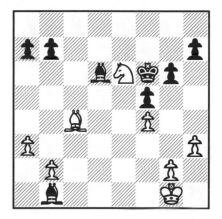

Camp Test Position 7
Black to move

56

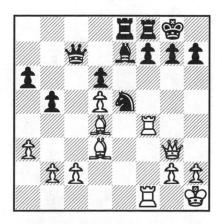

Camp Test Position 8
White to move

57

Camp Test Position 9
White to move

58

Camp Test Position 10
Black to move

59

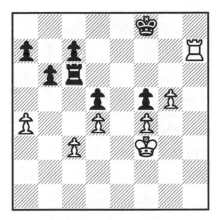

Camp Test Position 11
White to move

60

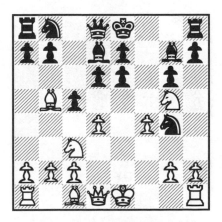

Camp Test Position 12
Black to move

61

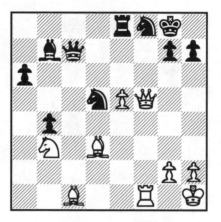

Camp Test Position 13
White to move

62

Camp Test Position 14
White to move

63

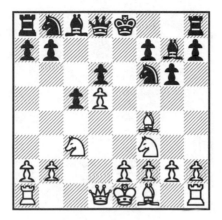

Camp Test Position 15
White to move

64

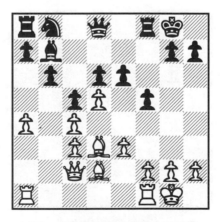

Camp Test Position 16
Black to move

65

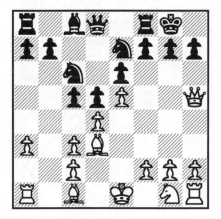

Camp Test Position 17
Black to move

66

Camp Test Position 18
White to move

67

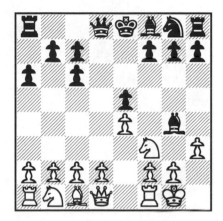

Camp Test Position 19
Black to move

68

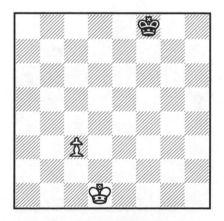

Camp Test Position 20
White to move

69

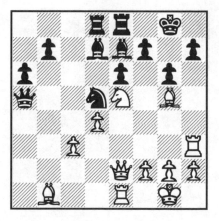

Camp Test Position 21
White to move

70

Camp Test Position 22
Black to move

71

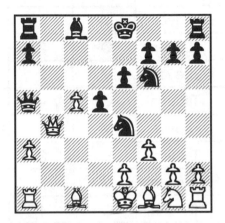

Camp Test Position 23
Black to move

72

Camp Test Position 24
White to move

Solution Key to Camp Test 1995

Position Number	Side to Move	Position Type	Phase of Game	Level of Difficulty	Solution
1.	B	Tactical	E	4	1. ... Kc8
2.	W	Lever	M	3	1. h5
3.	B	Lever	O	2	1. ... c5
4.	W	Lever	M	2	1. e4
5.	W	Tactical	O	4	1. Nxe6
6.	W	Lever	M	2	1. h5
7.	B	Tactical	E	3	1. ... b5
8.	W	Tactical	M	3	1. Bxh7 +
9.	W	Tactical	O	4	1. Nc3
10.	B	Tactical	M	2	1. ... Rc5
11.	W	Tactical	E	3	1. Kg3
12.	B	Tactical	O	3	1. ... Bxb5
13.	W	Tactical	M	3	1. Nc5
14.	W	Lever	E	2	1. Kc3
15.	W	Tactical	O	3	1. Qa4 +
16.	B	Lever	M	4	1. ... g6
17.	B	Tactical	O	3	1. ... Ng6
18.	W	Tactical	E	2	1. Ke5
19.	B	Tactical	O	2	1. ... h5
20.	W	Tactical	E	3	1. Kc2
21.	W	Tactical	M	4	1. Nxf7 or 1. Rxh7
22.	B	Tactical	E	4	1. Rc1 + , 1. Rc2, 1. Rc3
23.	B	Tactical	O	3	1. ... Qc7
24.	W	Lever	E	4	1. c4

Max = 72

Discussion: The Camp Test 1995

This is intended to be the most difficult comprehensive test that we are presenting. We believe that it thereby represents a good cross-section of the type of knowledge that the strongest players today must be able to access. The test was developed for Kopec's Chess Camp at the Pomfret School in the summer of 1995 where it was tested on a small group of subjects ranging from Class B to Expert. Results are reported in Appendix 3. This chapter represents an extension of the ideas developed in the earlier chapters. Up to now the main concepts that have been represented in the first two test sets are levers and tactics. All positions fell into one of these two categories. Now we extend upon these two general ideas and add the notion of the three phases of play: openings, middlegames, and endings. The examples represent a quantum leap in difficulty because of the breadth of topics tested and the very nature of the positions themselves.

The opening positions presented are sharp, theoretical and very specific. That is, you must have specific knowledge of the openings from which these positions have been derived. Finding the correct move in a given position essentially means knowing the opening sequence of moves which led to the position as well as the unique necessary move in the position. These positions are sharp like a razor's edge and if the proper move is not found, immediate bloodshed can result. To some degree it is arguable that finding the indicated move in these difficult positions is a matter of chess erudition. As we have discussed with regard to the Bratko-Kopec Test, the amount of chess erudition (or knowledge and experience) which a person has will correlate to his/her understanding and ability to find the correct or best moves in a position. The opening positions in this test are by and large based on theoretical knowledge which has been accrued during the past ten to twenty years. More than twenty years ago, these positions were hardly known — at least in terms of the necessary best move. For computer programs the opening positions are also challenging in that they require *a priori* opening book library inclusion. Finding moves like . . . c5 in position 52, Nc3 in position 57, . . . Bxb5 in position 59, and 1. Qa4+ Bd7 2. Qb3 in position 63 would not come automatically to them. Likewise computer programs would need to have considerable theoretical knowledge to play . . . h5 in position 67 and . . . Qc7 (a long piece sacrifice in the Nimzo-Indian) in position 71.

In summary, the opening positions are generally hard, specific, sharp, and challenging. As a whole they represent a quantum increase in difficulty in this test set.

The eight middlegame positions involve various original implementations of the notions of levers and diverse tactical motifs. Some of the concepts illustrated are: the attacking lever, central lever for counterplay against a wing attack, use of pawn majorities, exploiting overloaded pieces, original forms of well known attacking themes, sweeping, sealing,"intermezzo" checks, and more.

Finally the endgame positions test a wide range of themes including very specific rook and pawn ending knowledge, conversion of material advantages, triangulation in king and pawn endings, and long-range planning.

Scoring

Scoring for the CampTest 1995 is done in the same way as for the previous two test sets except that now there is one more parameter to measure: performance in the different phases of play; namely openings, middlegames, and endings. That is why we have deliberately selected eight positions from each phase of play. Thus, this test gives scores based on six measures: levers, tactics, overall score, openings, middlegames, endings and level of difficulty. Note that among these twenty-four positions there are only seven classified as lever positions.

Complete Solutions for the Camp Test 1995

49

1. ... Kc8 [1. ... Ke8 2. Re7+ Kd8 3. Rh7! with the difference that now, with the White rook on the h-file, Black cannot get "checking distance" on that side.

Camptest Position 1
Lasker, 1925
Black to move

3. ... Kc8 (3. ... Ke8 4. Rh8+ Kf7 5. Kd7 Ra1 6. d6) 4. Rh8+ Kb7 5. Kd7 Rg1 (5. ... Rc7+ 6. Ke6 Rg7 7. d6) 6. d6 Rg7+ (6. ... Rg2 7. Kd8) 7. Ke6 Rg6+ 8. Ke7 Rg7+ 9. Kf6] 2. **Rg8+** [2. Rh7 Rg1 3. Ke6 Re1+ 4. Kd6 Rg1] 2. ... **Kb7 3. Kd7 Rh1! 4. Rg7** [lf 4. d6 Rh7+ 5. Ke6 Rh6+ 6. Ke7 Rh7+ and Black draws because he has "checking distance" between his rook and the White pawn.] **4. ... Rh8 5. d6 Kb6=**

50

Attacking with pawns:

1. h5!! exd3 2. h6! with a big advantage due to his superior pawn structure and due to Black's weakened kingside dark squares.

Camptest Position 2
Timman-Miles
Netherlands vs. England, 1977
World Chess Title Contenders and Their Styles, p. 50
White to move

51

Camptest Position 3
Pirc Austrian with h4

Black to move

After 1. e4 d6 2. d4 Nf6 3. Nc3 g6 4. f4 Bg7 5. Nf3 0-0 6. e5 Nfd7 7. h4, it is important that Black respond to White's wing assault with an immediate counterattack in the center: **7. ... c5**

52

Camptest Position 4
Marshall-Capablanca
New York, 1909

Lasker's Manual
White to move

Classic planning example: Marshall had White and did not realize his correct plan for play — **1. e4** followed by **2. Qe3, f4** and kingside pawn mobilization. Instead he soon ended up trading queens and lost an endgame which has become a hallmark example of how to win with an outside majority

53

Camptest Position 5
Winawer French,
Qd7 line (Valvo)

White to move

1. e4 e6 2. d4 d5 3. Nc3 Bb4 4. e5 Qd7 5. a3 Bxc3+ 6. bxc3 b6 7. Qg4 f5 8. Qg3 Ba6 9. Bxa6 Nxa6 10. Ne2 Nb8 11. Nf4 Nc6 and Black's queen is overloaded.

Thus:

12. Nxe6. A series of 1989 articles by IM Mike Valvo, IM John Watson and GM Ian Rogers in *Inside Chess* led to the conclusion that **12. ... Qxe6 13. Qxg7 Qg6 14. Qxh8** favors White since Black is unable to trap the White queen.

54

White probes the light squares: **1. h5!** This lever pressured Black into playing ... g5 and weakening the critical kingside light squares.

Camptest Position 6
Kopec-Bellin
Edinburgh Congress, 1981
White to move

55

Excellent example of decoy and undermining using the power of the two bishops. **1. ... b5 2. Bb3** (2. Bd5 Be4 3. Bb3 Bd3 transposes) **2. ... Bd3!** with the idea of Bc4! when the

Camptest Position 7
Bessor-Hort
Halle, 1966
The Best Move, #49
Black to move

White knight will be left stranded. A variation could now go: **3. g3 Bc4 4. Bxc4 bxc4 5. Nd8** (5. Ng5 Bxa3-+) **5. ... Bxa3!-+**.

56

Camptest Position 8
Bednarski-Adamski
Slupsk, 1978
Chess Informant 26
(Combination #11)
White to move

A surprise tactical blow, with an original form of the Bxh7 sacrifice:

1. Bxh7+! Kxh7 2. Rxf7 Rxf7 3. Rxf7 and Black has no defense.

57

Camptest Position 9
Ruy Lopez,
Schliemann Variation
White to move

This position arises after 1. e4 e5 2. Nf3 Nc6 3. Bb5 f5 4. d4 fxe4 5. Nxe5 Nxe5 6. dxe5 c6. White sacrifices a piece for a strong initiative: **7. Nc3! cxb5 8. Nxe4 d5 9. exd6 Nf6 10. Qd4** with a dangerous attack.

58

Camptest Position 10
Ree-Jansa
Cracow, 1964
The Best Move, #33
Black to move

Rook lift to get all your pieces into the attack:

1. ... Rc5! 2. Rf1 Ne3!!-+.

59

The classic example of the active king in rook and pawn endings. **1. Kg3 Rxc3+ 2. Kh4 Rf3** (2. ... Rc1 [a better try according to Fine] 3. g6 *[better is 3. Kh5]* and now a sample line is 3. ... Rh1+ *[3. ... Rg1 4. Kh5]* 4. Kg5 Rxh7 5. gxh7 Kg7 6. Kxf5 Kxh7 7. Ke5 c6 8. Kd6 b5 9. axb5 cxb5 10. Kxd5 b4 11. Kc4 a5 12. d5 Kg6 13. d6 Kf6 14. f5 Kf7=) **3. g6 Rxf4+ 4. Kg5 Re4 5. Kf6! Kg8 6. Rg7+ Kh8 7. Rxc7 Re8 8. Kxf5 Re4 9. Kf6 Rf4+ 10. Ke5 Rg4 11. g7+ Kg8 12. Rxa7 Rg1 13. Kxd5+-.**

Camptest Position 11
Capablanca-Tartakower
New York, 1924
White to move

60

In this sharp variation of the Pirc-Austrian Attack, stemming from 1. e4 d6 2. d4 Nf6 3. Nc3 g6 4. f4 Bg7 5. Nf3 c5 6. Bb5+ Bd7 7. e5 Ng4 8. e6 fxe6 9. Ng5, Black has the surprising draw with:

1. ... Bxb5!! e.g. **2. Nxe6 Bxd4 3. Nxd8 Bf2+** and Black has a perpetual check.

Camptest Position 12
Pirc Austrian early ... c5
Black to move

61

CampTest Position 13
Pritchett-Georghiu
London, 1980
Mastering Chess, p. 105
White to move

Fueling the attack:
1. Nc5 Bc8 (1. ... Qxc5?? 2.Qf7+) and play concluded **2. Qf3 Nb6** (the c5-knight and the e-pawn are still immune) **3. e6!** (Now on 3. ... Bxe6 4. Qxf8+! etc., or on 3. ... Nxe6 4. Bxh7+! wins) **3. ... Rd8 4. Bg5 1-0.**

62

Camptest Position 14
Lasker-Bogaltyrshuk
Moscow, 1935
Pawn Power in Chess
(Diagram #145)
White to move

A famous position which exemplifies the idea of "sealing" (Kmoch). **1. Kc3** with the idea of **Kd4** followed by **e4** and White wins. Instead, after 1. e4?? d4 White had no

way to break through. Refer to *Lasker's Manual* or *Pawn Power* for more details about the ensuing ending.

63

Camptest Position 15
Portisch-Fischer
Palma de Mallorca, 1970
White to move

This Benoni position occurred after 1. d4 Nf6 2. c4 e6 3. Nf3 c5 4. d5 exd5 5. cxd5 g6 6. Nc3 Bg7 7. Bf4 d6. Portisch then played **8. Qa4+.** The idea behind this move is to cause confusion in Black's ranks. In this position Lubojevic (against Korchnoi) has even played **8. ... Ke7?!** with the idea of castling by hand after ... Re8 to follow. **8. ... Bd7 9. Qb3±.** Modern Benoni theory has advanced much further from the diagrammed position.

64

Wyvill formation (Nimzo-Indian); exceptional example. White is unable to exploit the weakened Black kingside dark squares. **1. ... g6!** with the idea that if **2. dxe6** Qf6 then **3. e4 f4** and Black succeeds in

Camptest Position 16
Kopec-Fluk
New York City
High School
Championships,
1969-70
Mastering Chess
pp. 47-48
Black to move

keeping the position closed. If instead 1. ... Qf6 then 2. e4 f4 3. e5 would give White some chances.

65

This position is reached via:

1. e4 e6 2. d4 d5 3. Nc3 Bb4 4. e5 c5 5. a3 Bxc3+ 6. bxc3 Ne7 7. Qg4 0-0 8. Bd3 Nbc6 9. Qh5. In this unclear variation of the French Defense (where Black has castled very early) **9. ... Ng6** is now the only reasonable try.

Camptest Position 17
French Winawer,
Qg4 variation
Black to move

66

Camptest Position 18
Mastering Chess p. 88
White to move

Triangulation in order to achieve the opposition. The idea is that if White can achieve the same position with Black to move, then White will win. **1. Ke5 Kc6 2. Kd4 Kd7 3. Kd5** (opposition) **3. ... Kc8** (3. Ke7 4. c6) **4. Ke6** (4. Kd6 Kd8 5. c6 Kc8 6. Kc5 Kb8=) **4. ... Kb8 5. Kd7 Ka8 6. c6+/-.**

67

Camptest Position 19
Ruy Lopez Exchange
5. ... Bg4
Black to move

The Ruy Lopez Exchange Variation arising from 1. e4 e5 2. Nf3 Nc6 3. Bb5 a6 4. Bxc6 dxc6 5. 0-0 Bg4 6. h3. Now the correct move is:

6. ... h5. It is important that Black knows this move — a piece sacrifice that White cannot accept. After 6. ... Bxf3 7. Qxf3 Black would be without his two bishop potential and would have no compensation for his doubled pawns, while 6. ... Bh5 can simply be met by 7. g4 Bg6 8. Nxe5 when Black cannot recapture on e4 and finds himself a pawn down with insufficient compensation.

68

1. Kc2! All other moves only draw. The idea is to advance the rank of the White king while maximizing the file distance between the White king and Black king. Thus, 1. ... Ke7 2. Kb3 Kd6 3. Kb4+-. However, if 1. Kd2 Ke7, then 2. Kd3 Kd7=.

Camptest Position 20
Endgame Study
Advances in Computer Chess 1
(M. Clarke), 1977
White to move

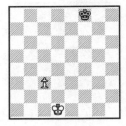

69

The sacrificial explosion. **1. Nxf7!!** 1. Rxh7 also works because if 1. ... Nxc3 then 2. Qf3 is winning for White. **1. ... Bxg5** (1. ... Kxf7 2. Rxh7+ Kg8 3. Qe4+-; 1. ... Nxc3 2. Qd2 [Browne]) **2. Rxh7!!** There are many complicated lines here, all

Camptest Position 21
Browne-Zuckerman
New York, 1973
World Chess Titled Contenders and Their Styles pp. 67-68
White to move

favoring White. **2. ... Nf6** (2. ... Nf4 3. Qg4 Qxc3 4. Rf1 Qc4 *[4. ... Kxh7 5. Nxg5+ Kg7 6. Qxf4 Rf8 7. Qe5+ Kh6 8. Qe4+-]* 5. Qxg5 Kxh7 6. Qxf4 Kg7 7. Ne5 Rf8 8. Qg5 Qxf1+ 9. Kxf1 Bb5+ 10. Ke1+-) **3. Bxg6 Nxh7 4. Qh5 Qxc3 5. Qxh7+ Kf8 6. Rf1 Qxd4 7. Ne5 Qf4 8. Nxd7+.** Better is 8. Bh5! Qf6 9. Ng6+ Qxg6 10. Bxg6, and mate next (Fritz3). But Browne was in time pressure. **8. ... Rxd7 9. Qh8+ Ke7 10. Qxe8+** and White wins.

70

Camptest Position 22
Mastering Chess
p. 123, #24
Black to move

A classic example of the importance of the active rook. **1. ... Rc1+** (1. ... Ra8? places the rook passively, which would ultimately lose for Black.) **2. Kh2 Kg6 3. Rxa5 Ra1** when Black's active rook secures a draw. 1. ... Rc2 or 1. ... Rc3 also draw with the same idea as Rc1.

71

Camptest Position 23
Nimzo Indian,
Qc2 Piece Sac
Black to move

This unusual position arises after the Classical Variation (4. Qc2) of the Nimzo Indian Defense: 1. d4 Nf6 2. c4 e6 3. Nc3 Bb4 4. Qc2 c5 5. dxc5 Na6 6. a3 Bxc3+ 7. Qxc3 Nxc5 8. b4 Nce4 9. Qd4 d5 10. c5 b6 11. f3 Black must now sacrifice — or lose — a piece. 11. ... bxc5 12. bxc5 Qa5+ 13. Qb4 and now Black gets maximum pressure for the piece by **13. ... Qc7! 14. fxe4 Rb8 15. Qa4+ Bd7 16. c6 Qe5!** (A 1993 novelty. The original Ivanchuk-deFirmian game went 16. ... 0-0 17. Bd2! Bxc6 when White was able to survive) **17. cxd7+ Ke7** when Black has full compensation for the sacrificed material. This piece sacrifice was introduced by GM Nick de Firmian vs. GM Vassily Ivanchuk at the 1990 Manila Interzonal. This variation stemming from 4. Qc2 has helped effect the re-emergence of the entire system for White in recent years.

72

Overall, we believe this is an excellent example of planning and pawn play. We have essentially presented Lasker's commentary here in the notes to 1. ... c6. **1. c4! a5** [1. ... c6 The game continuation. 2. g4?

Camptest Position 24
MacDonnell-Lewis
Lasker's Manual p. 174
White to move

Too soon. (First 2. b4 was indicated, when White wins because the pin is unbreakable. If ... d5 then 3. c5) **A)** 2. ... a5 3. a3 *(3. b3 is too late: ... b6 4. a3 d5)* 3. ... a4 followed by ... b6 and ... d5.; **B)** 2. ... d5 Black does not grasp the opportunity. 3. c5 b6 4. b4 d4 5. Re5 bxc5 6. bxc5 a6 7. Kf2 Rf8 8. Ke2 White wins the d-pawn and the game easily.] **2. b3 b6 3. a3 c6 4. b4 axb4 5. axb4 d5 6. c5 bxc5 7. bxc5 d4 8. g4** [Not 8. Kf2? Rf8; Also 8. Re4? d3 9. Rd4+ Kc7 10. Bxe6 Rxe6 11. Rxd3 Re5 12. Rc3 *(12. Rh3 h5)* 12. ... Kb7!=] **8. ... d3 9. Kf2 d2 10. Rd1 Kc7 11. Bxe6 Rxe6 12. Rxd2+-** White still seems to be winning. This analysis has included contributions from GM Lubomir Ftacnik.

Chapter 3

The Rook and Pawn Test

Discussion: The Rook and Pawn Endings Test

This chapter introduces a new way to look at all multi-pawn rook endings. We estimate that rook and pawn endings may occur as frequently as in one out of six games. That is, if one of three games amongst equal-strength players results in an endgame, and if half of all endings are rook and pawn endings (as generally accepted) then 1/3 times 1/2 would yield 1/6. *Voila* — one in six games may end with rook and pawn endings. People have tried to study and teach the correct play of rook and pawn endings from many perspectives. One hears about active rooks, rooks behind passed pawns, active kings, passed pawns, good pawn structures, bad pawn structures, outside passed pawns, pawn majorities, etc., but what does it all mean? Our observation has been that most writers and students are too interested in finding and defining individual "best moves" as opposed to defining and understanding the pervasive or dominant themes in any position. That is our purpose here — to present and identify the three major pervasive concepts which hierarchically define the status and correct play of all general rook and multi-pawn endings.

Really, how can you talk about the best move in any chess position before you can demonstrate that you understand it? Any chess position should first be understood statically — that is, what are the current features of the position? Namely, the material, the king safety, the piece activity, the identifiable strengths and weaknesses, such as powerful or weak pawn structures and piece configurations, etc. Then we can consider strong moves and groups of moves (combinations) which may force a transformation to a stronger (better) position. In other words, a position can first be viewed from a strategical (long term) perspective, and then from a tactical (short term) perspective. The "bridge" between tactical and strategical considerations may defined as a "combination". Combinations in chess can be deemed to fall into four categories, including combinations which: (1) force mate, (2) gain material, (3) force a draw, and (4) improve one's position.

In this chapter we are concerned with rook and multi-pawn endings where there is a definite advantage for one side, but the advantage will not be in terms of material. It will be present in terms of only one of three possible factors: (1) better rook, (2) better pawns, or (3) better king. The correct play of any ending can be viewed as a combination which typically transforms one identifiable advantage to two advantages (better rook and better king; or better rook and better pawn structure; or better king and better pawn structure) or possibly all three identifiable advantages.

Here is a categorization for rook endings, developed by Danny Kopec. The type of advantage indicates which piece(s) plays the most significant role in providing a side with an advantage.

Category	Type of Advantage
0	None
1	Rook, Pawn, King
2	Rook, Pawn
3	Pawn, King
4	Rook, King
5	Rook
6	Pawn
7	King

For purposes of discussion here, all positions have material equality. At this time our database of rook and pawn endings has 45 positions (from which 35 have been selected for this test) illustrating this approach. Many positions can be tested as both White to move and Black to move. Here is an example of how one advantage can lead to two advantages and then to three advantages: a better rook ties up the opposing rook (Category 5). Then the king comes in for help

(Category 4); finally pawns are advanced to create a passed pawn or material is won (Category 1). Another example is: a passed pawn advantage (for example, Category 6). The rook moves behind the passed pawn and the weaker side's rook is forced into a defensive position in front of the pawn (Category 2); the White king comes in for decisive help. Thereby we have advantages of better king and rook and pawn (Category 1).

Whatever the category a position is in, the goal is to achieve Category 1. This may be viewed as a form of "window dressing" but such a demonstration is usually sufficient to get the strongest players to resign, i.e. *zugzwang* (usually resulting in imminent loss of material or checkmate) with no counterplay. Against weaker players it is a sure recipe for making progress (bridging) from one won position to another which is easier to handle. One of the underlying principles of this approach is that you never trade your advantage of an active rook for a new advantage, unless you can get two pawns ahead and/or can calculate a forced win. The point is that you don't want too many pawns to get traded via your opponent's active rook whereby both sides get passed pawns and the game becomes somewhat of a raffle. If it does deteriorate into a race of passed pawns, then make sure that it is a no contest race. For example, if you have the better rook, (that is, your opponent's rook is passive) you don't want to let your opponent also get an active rook after you win a pawn. In other words, an active rook is worth more than a pawn. However, if you can win two pawns which can quickly become passed, or if you can calculate (or see) an easy "no contest race" then you might enter such a transaction.

The real idea behind this approach is to build upon existing advantages leading to the constriction of your opponent's play and his/her options. Better rook, better pawns, better king = resigns.

The Rook and Pawn Test

Instructions for taking this test

You are allowed two minutes for each of the following positions. In each case determine the category (of the eight categories presented on the previous pages) of the position for the side to move and the best move. You should only select one move which you believe to be the correct or best move in the position. The correct category is worth one point and the correct move choice is worth two points. Therefore the maximum score on this test is 105 points (35 for the 35 positions and their categories, 70 for the 35 possible correct move choices). You will also receive a level of difficulty score, by summing the difficulty numbers on the solution sheet, for positions where you have selected the correct move. See the discussion of the BK Test for more on the interpretation of difficulty level scores.

Answer Sheet for Rook and Pawn Test

Position Number	Category	Best Move	Side to Move
1.			White
2.			White
3.			White
4.			White
5.			White
6.			White
7.			White
8.			White
9.			White
10.			Black
11.			White
12.			Black
13.			Black
14.			White
15.			White
16.			Black
17.			White
18.			White
19.			Black
20.			Black
21.			White
22.			White
23.			White
24.			White
25.			White
26.			White
27.			White
28.			Black
29.			White
30.			Black
31.			Black
32.			Black
33.			White
34.			White
35.			White

Reprise of the categories and the corresponding type of advantages: 0 = none; 1 = rook, pawn, king; 2 = rook, pawn; 3 = pawn, king; 4 = rook, king; 5 = rook; 6 = pawn; 7 = king.

73

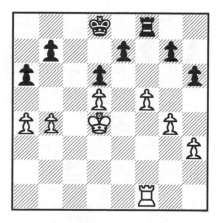

Rook and Pawn Position 1
White to move

74

Rook and Pawn Position 2
White to move

75

Rook and Pawn Position 3
White to move

76

Rook and Pawn Position 4
White to move

77

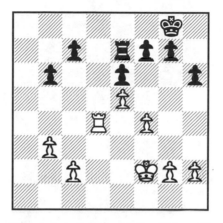

Rook and Pawn Position 5
White to move

78

Rook and Pawn Position 6
White to move

79

Rook and Pawn Position 7
White to move

80

Rook and Pawn Position 8
White to move

81

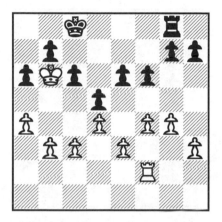

Rook and Pawn Position 9
White to move

82

Rook and Pawn Position 10
Black to move

83

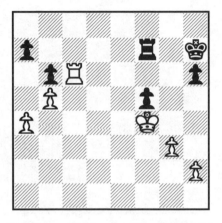

Rook and Pawn Position 11
White to move

84

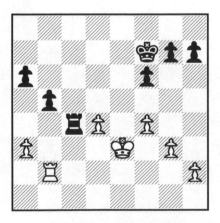

Rook and Pawn Position 12
Black to move

85

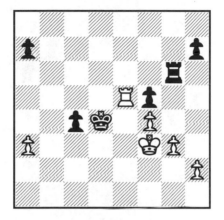

Rook and Pawn Position 13
Black to move

86

Rook and Pawn Position 14
White to move

87

Rook and Pawn Position 15
White to move

88

Rook and Pawn Position 16
Black to move

89

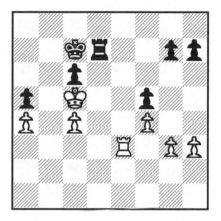

Rook and Pawn Position 17
White to move

90

Rook and Pawn Position 18
White to move

91

Rook and Pawn Position 19
Black to move

92

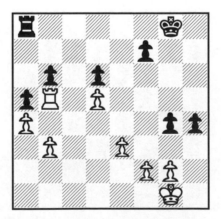

Rook and Pawn Position 20
Black to move

93

Rook and Pawn Position 21
White to move

94

Rook and Pawn Position 22
White to move

95

Rook and Pawn Position 23
White to move

96

Rook and Pawn Position 24
White to move

97

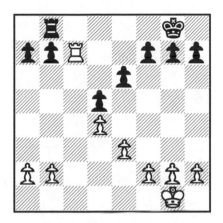

Rook and Pawn Position 25
White to move

98

Rook and Pawn Position 26
White to move

99

Rook and Pawn Position 27
White to move

100

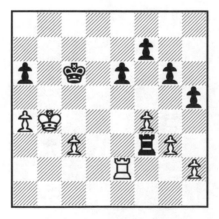

Rook and Pawn Position 28
Black to move

101

Rook and Pawn Position 29
White to move

102

Rook and Pawn Position 30
Black to move

103

Rook and Pawn Position 31
Black to move

104

Rook and Pawn Position 32
Black to move

105

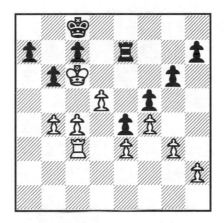

Rook and Pawn Position 33
White to move

106

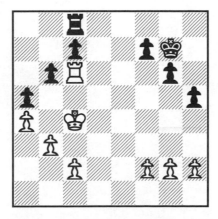

Rook and Pawn Position 34
White to move

107

Rook and Pawn Position 35
White to move

Solution Key to Rook and Pawn Test

Position Number	Side to Move	Category	Level of Difficulty	Solution
1.	W	1	4	1. b5
2.	W	2	2	1. Rf4
3.	W	3	3	1. Rf4
4.	W	4	3	1. Rc8 or 1. a4
5.	W	5	1	1. Rd8 +
6.	W	6	2	1. Kf2
7.	W	7	2	1. f5
8.	W	6	4	1. f5
9.	W	7	3	1. Re2
10.	B	0	2	1. ... g6
11.	W	1	2	1. h4
12	B	2	2	1. ... Ke6
13.	B	3	2	1. ... Ra6
14.	W	4	3	1. Kg3
15.	W	5	2	1. Rd8 +
16.	B	6	2	1. ... Re6
17.	W	7	1	1. Re6
18.	W	6	2	1. Rh3
19.	B	0	2	1. ... Re7
20.	B	0	3	1. ... Rc8
21.	W	1	2	1. g5
22.	W	2	2	1. Ke2
23.	W	3	3	1. b5
24.	W	4	1	1. Kb4
25.	W	5	2	1. Kf1
26.	W	2	2	1. Ra4
27.	W	7	1	1. Rc3
28.	B	4	2	1. ... h4
29.	W	2	1	1. Rc6
30.	B	0	2	1. ... e5
31.	B	2	2	1. ... Kd6
32.	B	1	2	1. ... Kc5
33.	W	3	1	1. c5
34.	W	4	3	1. Kb5
35.	W	5	2	1. Kg4

Max = 75

Complete Solutions for the Rook and Pawn Test

73

Category 1: better rook, king, and pawn.

White is clearly better; Black has backward pawns on e7 and g7. White has a superior king and a lot more space. White rook is

Rook and Pawn
Position 1
Danny Kopec, 1992
White to move

active, Black rook is passive. Black should not be allowed his rook on an open file. 1. Rc1 seems like the logical best move for White but Black has 1. ... h5!, creating an open file for his rook (h-file) and counterplay. A continuation might be 1. ... h5 2. Ke4 hxg4 3. hxg4 Rh8 and Black has strong counterplay. For this reason another approach is needed. 1. Ke4 is the next logical try, with the idea of meeting 1. ... h5 with 2. g5. This approach just barely falls short, a fact not discovered by the authors until deep into the analysis of the position. We then went back to the drawing board and finally discovered a completely new idea:

1. b5!! This exploits further White's space advantage. (As mentioned above, we originally thought 1. Ke4 was best. The idea is to meet ... h5 with g5. A sample continuation could go 1. ... Kd7 *[if 1. ... h5 2. g5 Kd7 3. Rc1 when Black cannot play ... Rc8 as he would lose the h5-pawn in the king and pawn ending. 3. ... Rh8 4. g6!? Rf8 5. Kf4 Rg8 6. Kg5 Rh8 7. h4 Rh6 8. b5 with the idea of 9. b6 and 10. Rc7 or 8. ... axb5 9. axb5 b6 10. Rc6]* 2. Rc1 Rc8 *[a passive move like 2. ... Rg8?*

would eventually lose]). After 2. ... Rc8, the king and pawn ending is better for White but it seems Black can barely hold 3. Rxc8 Kxc8. We will not give all the variations here — they are very complex and would fill pages! The reader can work them out for himself using the following "candidate" moves as a starting point. If any reader thinks he can prove that there is a win in the king and pawn ending, we would like to hear about it. Fortunately, the main line wins so convincingly that there is no need for the king and pawn ending to be won as well.

(a) 4. f6!? The idea is to infiltrate on the light squares. 4. ... gxf6 *(4. ... exf6? 5. Kf5 Kd7 6. Kg6 Ke7 7. Kxg7+-)* 5. Kf5 Kd7=;

(b) 4. Kf4 with two ways of continuing:

(b1) He plays h4 and g5; on ... hxg5 he can take back either with the king or the pawn. Both seem to fall short of a win against best play.

(b2) He tries Kg3-h4-h5 first, then thinks about h4 and g5. This also fails to win. 4. ... Kd8 and so on.

The main solution after 1. b5 continues: **1. ... axb5.**

1. ... a5? 2. b6 and White will win all king and pawn endings.

2. axb5 Kd7.

2. ... Kc7? 3. Rc1+ and then

(a) 3. ... Kb6 4. Re1 Re8 5. Kc4 Rc8+ 6. Kb4 Rc5 *(6. ... Rc7 7. Re6 Rd7 — 7 ... Rc5 transposes — 8. Rg6 Rc7 9. Rxg7)* 7. Rxe7 Rxd5 8. Rxg7 h5 9. f6 hxg4

(a1) 10. f7 Rd4+ 11. Kc3 Rf4 12. hxg4 d5 *(12. ... Kxb5 13. Rg5+ Kc6 14. Rf5)* 13. g5 Kxb5 14. g6+-;

(a2) 10. hxg4 10. ... Rxb5+ 11. Kc4 Rb1 12. f7 Rf1 13. g5 Kc6 14. g6+-;

(b) 3. ... Kd7 4. b6 Rc8 5. Ra1+-

3. Ra1 h5

3. ... Kc7 4. Rc1+! Kd7 *(4. ... Kb6 5. Re1 Re8 6. Kc4 Rc8+ 7. Kb4 transposes to (a) above)* 5. b6.

4. b6 hxg4 5. hxg4 Rh8 6. Ke4+-.

74

Category 2: better pawns and rook.

A rook behind an outside passed pawn wins. This is a famous example: **1. Rf4 b4 2. b3 Rf7 3. f6 Kd6 4. Kd4 Ke6 5. Rf2 Kd6 6. Ra2! Rc7 7. Ra6+ Kd7 8. Rb6.** White has now repositioned his rook and will gain the active king in addition.

Rook and Pawn
Position 2
Lasker-Rubinstein
St. Petersburg, 1914
Rook Endings, #203
White to move

75

Category 3: better king and pawns.

Black threatens to free himself with ... h5. Therefore **1. Rf4!** to meet ... h5 with gh. So play might continue: **1. ... Rh7 2. h4 h5 3. Ke3** etc. White has better pawn structure and chances of an outside passed pawn.

Rook and Pawn
Position 3
Danny Kopec, 1992
White to move

The passive defense 2. ... Rg7 might be a better try but then White can use his space advantage to prepare a pawn break on the queenside (such as c5), opening a file when only he is in a position to occupy it.

76

Rook and Pawn
Position 4
Danny Kopec, 1992
White to move

Category 4: better rook and king.

1. Rc8 Another way is: 1. a4 bxa4 2. Ra5 Kc6 (*2. ... Ra7? 3. b5 Kc7 4. Kc5+-*) 3. Rxa4 Kb5 4. Ra5+ Kb6 (*4 ... Kxb4 5. Rxa6 Re7 6. Ke5+-*) 5. Ke5+- **1. ... Ra7** Idea ... a5, activating the rook.

[1 ... Rc7? 2. Rxc7 Kxc7 3. Kc5+-] **2. Rd8+!** Drives back the king and spreads confusion in the ranks. **2. ... Ke7 3. Rb8** now Black has many ways to go. **3. ... a5** is the main line. Other possibilities are:

(a) 3. ... Kd6 4. Rb6+ Ke7 5. Ke5+-;

(b) 3. ... Rc7 4. Rb6 Rc2 5. Ke5! Rxg2 6. Rb7+ Kd8 7. Kxe6 Re2 8. Kd6 Kc8 9. Rxg7 Rxe3 10. Rg3. White's superior king will carry the day, e.g. 10. ... Re2 11. Rh3 d4 12. Kd5 Re3 13. Rg3 Re2 14. Rg8+ Kb7 15. Rg7+ Kb6 16. Rxh7 Ra2 17. h4 Rxa3 18. Kxd4 Rb3 19. Rh6+ Kb7 20. Kc5 Rxd3 21. Rh7+ Kc8 22. h5 Rf3 23. h6 Rxf4 24. Ra7 Rh4 25. h7+-.

4. Rxb5 axb4 5. axb4 Ra2 6. Ke5 Rxg2 7. Rb7+ Kd8 8. Kxe6 Re2 9. Kd6+- White has reached a Category 1 position.

77

Category 5: better rook.

The better rook should win, e.g **1. Rd8+ Kh7 2. Ke3** etc. Black to move can neutralize the White rook with the maneuver 1. ... Kf8-e8-Rd7 etc. (=). If

Rook and Pawn Position 5
Danny Kopec, 1992
White to move

Black tries the lever ... g5, then after fxg5 hxg5, the White king goes to g4 when the g5-pawn can be proven weak. White also has possibilities of an outside passed pawn after ... g5, fxg5, hxg5, the White king moves to g4 and then the pawns advance to g3 and h4. Ideally, White will want to keep the Black king confined on the kingside while he infiltrates on the queenside. This is not so easy to accomplish if Black plays a timely ... f6 (his best defense).

78

Category 6: better pawns.

1. Kf2. White must keep the Black rook out to avoid counterplay. This also activates the king and offers later opportunities to swap rooks.

Rook and Pawn Position 6
Danny Kopec, 1992
White to move

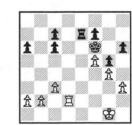

79

Rook and Pawn
Position 7
Danny Kopec, 1992

White to move

Category 7: better king.
White actually has better pawns and better rook too. His pawns and rook are better due to space and mobility. However, better king is the dominating factor. **1. f5** Black cannot avoid an opening of the position favorable to White.

80

Rook and Pawn
Position 8
Danny Kopec, 1992

White to move

Category 6: better pawns.

White's only advantage is the better pawn-structure: outside passed pawn and backward Black d-pawn.

1. f5! Note that by first increasing his space advantage on the king-side, White enhances his chances of winning on either wing. White threatens 2. Rd4 followed by 3. Re4 when in any race he has an extra tempo on the kingside. (Unclear is 1. Rd4 Re1 2. Re4 Rb1 3. f5 Rb3+ 4. Kf4 Rxh3 5. Re7 Rb3 6. Rxf7 Rxb4+ 7. Kg3 Rc4 8. Rxg7 b4. Somewhat surprisingly, despite his greatly superior queenside pawn structure, White cannot win directly by 1. a6 Ra8 2. Ra1 etc.) **1. ... g6** (1. ... f6 2. Rd4) **2. fxg6 fxg6 3. Rd6+-.**

81

Category 7: better king.

(Note that the pawn structure is more balanced here than in position 7.)

Rook and Pawn Position 9
Danny Kopec, 1992
White to move

1. Re2 Threatening e4.
1. ... f5 2. Rg2! It is clear that after **2. ... g6 3. g5** followed by **h4-h5** and **Rh2** wins for White. Note that if Black tries 3. ... Rh8, then 4. h4 h5 5. gxh6 *e.p.* Rxh6 6. h5! still wins for White.

82

Category 0: no advantage.

With **1. ... g6**, Black ensures that he can follow with **2. ... Kf8** and **... Ke8** driving the White rook from the seventh rank. Then he can also challenge White's possession of the d-file.

Rook and Pawn Position 10
Pawn Power in Chess,
Diagram 105
Black to move

83

Rook and Pawn
Position 11
Levenfish - Lisitsyn
Moscow, 1935
Rook Endings, #274
White to move

Category 1: better rook, king and pawns.

White won by:

1. h4 Rg7 2. h5 Rg4+ (2. ... Rf7 3. Ke5 and Rf6) **3. Kxf5 Rxa4** (3. ... Rxg3 4. Rc7+ Kg8 5. Rxa7 Rg5+ 6. Kf6 Rxh5 7. a5! Rxb5 8. Rg7+ Kf8 9. a6+- with the idea of Rb7, a7, Ra8+.) **4. Rc7+ Kg8 5. Kg6 Rg4+ 6. Kxh6 Rxg3 7. Rxa7 Rb3 8. Rb7!** Although there have been many exchanges in the sequence which led to an active Black rook, White always maintained the better king coupled with the more dangerous pawns. Note also that the White rook is more effective as it confines the Black king to the back rank. **8. ... Rxb5 9. Kg6 Kf8 10. h6 Re5** (10. ... Rb1 11. Rb8+ Ke7 12. h7) **11. Rb8+ 1-0.**

84

Rook and Pawn
Position 12
Marshall - Chigorin
Barmen, 1905
Rook Endings, #266
Black to move

Category 2: better rook and pawns.

Black sets out to prove that White's d-pawn is not passed and strong but isolated and weak. Wrong is 1. ... Rc3+ 2. Ke4 Rxa3 3. Kd5 and "White's weak d-pawn becomes strong" (Averbakh and Smyslov). Black first improves his king with **1. ... Ke6!** The game continuation was 2. Rb3 Kd5 3. Rd3 f5 4. h3 h5 5. Ke2 Rxd4 and Black went on to win. A better try is 2. Ke4 f5+ 3. Kd3 when Black should not play 3. ... Kd5? 4. Rb4!, but instead 3. ... Ra4! 4. Rb3 Kd5 and wins.

85

Category 3: better king and pawns.

1. ... Ra6 2. Rxf5 Rxa3+ 3. Ke2 Ra2+ 4. Kd1 Rxh2 5. Rf7! This looks like a better try than the game continuation. (The game continuation was 5. Ra5 Kd3 6. Rd5+ Kc3 7. Ra5

Rook and Pawn Position 13
Pillsbury - Janowski
Budapest, 1896
Rook Endings #270
Black to move

Rd2+ 8. Kc1 Rd7 9. Ra3+ Kb4 10. Rf3 c3 11. f5 Kb3 12. f6 Rf7 13. g4 h6 14. Rf5 a6 15. Rf1 a5 16. Rf5 a4 and Black was winning, though he later went wrong and allowed a draw.) **5. ... a5 6. Ra7 Kd3!** As in the game. (6. ... Kc3 7. Rxa5 Rh1+ 8. Ke2 Kc2 9. f5 c3 10. f6) **7. Rd7+** (King moves are worse). **7. ... Kc3 8. Ke1** (with the idea of f5). This seems to be the toughest defense. (8. f5 Rf2 9. g4 a4 [9. ... h5 10. gxh5 Rxf5 11. h6 Rh5 12. h7 a4 also leads to a win.] 10. Ra7 Rg2 11. Ke1 [*11. Rxa4 Kd3 12. Ke1 c3-+*] 11. ... Rxg4 12. Rxa4 Rf4 is a winning position for Black, though there are still some complications.) **8. ... a4 9. Ra7** Forced, as f5 is too slow. **9. ... Kb3 10. Rb7+ Kc2 11. f5 a3 12. Ra7 Kb2 13. f6 Rh6 14. f7 Rf6 15. Kd1 a2 16. Rb7+ Kc3 17. Ra7 Kd3 18. Rd7+ Ke3 19. Re7+** (19. Ra7 Rxf7) **19. ... Kf3 20. Ra7 Kxg3 21. Rxa2 Rxf7** is winning for Black. We would like to acknowledge Jack Edelson for assistance in analyzing this position.

86

Category 4: better rook and king.

White creates a much superior king with **1. Kg3!** Black's rook is active too, but White's rook on the seventh also creates mating threats with the White king. Play

Rook and Pawn Position 14
Capablanca - Tartakower
New York, 1924
Rook Endings, #273
White to move

continued: **1. ... Rxc3+ 2. Kh4 Rf3 3. g6! Rxf4+ 4. Kg5 Re4 5. Kf6!** and White regains his sacrificed pawns through his active rook and continuous mate threats. For more analysis, see the solution to Camp Test #11.

87

Rook and Pawn
Position 15
Danny Kopec, 1992
White to move

Category 5: better rook.

Black to move can pretty much secure a draw with 1. ... e5! followed by 2. ... Kf8-e7-Rd7. However, after **1. Rd8+ Kh7 2. f4** White has winning chances due to better rook, better pawns (space), and chances for the better King position.

88

Rook and Pawn
Position 16
Schlechter - Rubinstein
San Sebastian, 1912
Rook Endings, #267
Black to move

Category 6: better pawns.

White has three islands and Black has two. The superior pawn structure is turned into a superior rook. White's rook must defend the weak pawns.

1. ... Re6! ties the White rook to the weak pawns. Black can follow with ... Re4 and Rh4, then activate his king and advance his pawns. Attacking a weak pawn with your rook is a sure way to achieve the better rook — and that is always an important step in the winning process.

89

**Category 7:
better king.**

Domination
and a target;
1. Re6 wins quickly.

Rook and Pawn
Position 17
Danny Kopec, 1992
White to move

90

**Category 6:
better pawns.**

White has several
threats to win using
his protected passed
d-pawn. The main
threat is **1. Rh3** (or 1.
Rg3 g6 2. Rh3), but a4-
b5 with Rb3 is also a
threat.

Rook and Pawn
Position 18
Danny Kopec, 1992
White to move

91

**Category 0:
no advantage**

1. ... Re7 is Black's
only move because it
is necessary to prevent
White's rook from get-
ting to the seventh
rank.

Rook and Pawn
Position 19
Danny Kopec, 1995
Black to move

92

Rook and Pawn
Position 20
Danny Kopec, 1995
Black to move

**Category 0:
no advantage.**

1. ... Rc8 This is a certain kind of category 0 position where Black obtains an active rook and this is the only way to attain equality. A possible continuation would be:

2. Rxb6 (If instead 1. ... g3 2. Rxb6 Rc8 3. Rc6 Rb8 4. Rc3+-) **Rc1+ 3. Kh2 Rc2 4. Rxd6 Kg7!** This move prevents Rh6 which would help to eliminate Black's main trump — the threats of advancing his g- and h-pawns. In this position, despite being two pawns down, Black's active rook on the seventh and advanced kingside pawns seem to offer sufficient counterplay to draw. **5. Rc6.** Here is a sample variation which illustrates how tricky the position is for both sides: **5. ... Rxf2 6. Kg1** (Black threatened ... h3) **6. ... Rb2 7. Rc4 g3 8. Kf1 Rf2+ 9. Ke1 Rxg2 10. Rxh4 f5 11. Rh3** White must deal with the dangerous g-pawn before doing anything else. (11. d6? Rg1+ 12. Ke2 g2 13. Kf2 Rh1-+) **11. ... Kf6** (11. ... Rg1+ 12. Ke2 g2 13. Kf2 Rh1 14. Rg3+) **12. Kf1 Rf2+ 13. Kg1 Rb2 14. Rxg3 Rxb3 15. Kf2 Ke5=.**

93

Category 1: better rook, pawn, and king.

White's Pawns are better because of space. White uses the "widening bridge"(a term from *Rook Endings*) to win. That is:

Rook and Pawn
Position 21
Bernstein-Forgacz
Coburg, 1904
Rook Endings, #278
White to move

1. g5 hxg5 2. Kxg5 Rd7 3. h6 gxh6+ 4. Rxh6 Kg7 5. Rg6+ Kf7 6. Kf5 Ra7

6. ... Rd8 7. Rh6 Kg7 8. Rf6!± Rd7 9. Ke6 and then

(a) 9. ... Ra7 10. Rf4 Ra6 11. Rf7+ Kg6 12. Rc7 Ra4 *(12. ... Rb6 13. Rc6 Rb4 14. Kxd6 Rxc4 15. Rxc5+-)* 13. Kxd6 Rxc4 14. Rxc5+-;

(b) 9. ... Rd8 10. Rf7+ Kg6 11. Rd7+-

7. Rh6 Kg7 8. Rxd6 Ra4 9. Ke6 Rxc4 10. Rc6+-.

94

Category 2: Better rook and pawn.

A very famous position whereby White wins due to "island theory". White has two pawn islands versus Black's three and White can exploit this with his active rook. The Black rook is kept

Rook and Pawn
Position 22
Flohr - Vidmar
Nottingham, 1936
Rook Endings, #286
White to move

tied up defending pawns. An important motif is the creation of a new front of attack after the White king is centralized. The game sequence is extremely instructive. **1. Ke2 Ke7 2. Kd3 Kd6 3. Ra5**

Ra8 4. Kd4 f5 5. b4 Rb8? Better is 5. ... Kc7 in order to transfer the king to b6 and free the rook. 6. Kc5 *(6. e4 dxe4 7. fxe4 fxe4 8. Kxe4 Kb6 a move ahead of what he could have had in the game)* 6. ... Kb7 *(6. ... Rb8 7. a4!)* 7. Kd6 Re8 8. Ra3 d4! 9. exd4 Re2 10. Rc3 Rxg2 11. Rxc6, Rxh2 12. a4 g5! with equality. 6. a3 Ra8 7. e4! dxe4 8. fxe4 fxe4 9. Kxe4 Ra7? Black continues with passive defense when 9. ... Kc7 offered better chances to liberate his rook and seek active counterplay: 9. ... Kc7 10. Re5! Kb6 11. Re7 a5! with counterplay. 12. Rxh7 axb4 13. axb4 Ra4 14. Rg7 Rxb4+ 15. Kf3 etc., as given by Smyslov and Levenfish. 10. Kf4 h6 To prevent king entry but White now wins by Kg4 and h4-h5, exploiting the weakened kingside. 11. h4 Ke6 12. Kg4 Ra8 13. h5 g5 (13. ... gxh5+ 14. Kxh5 Rg8 15. g4! Kd6 16. Rxa6+-) 14. g3 Ra7 15. Kf3 Ra8 16. Ke4 Ra7 17. Re5+! Kd6 18. Re8 c5 19. Rd8+! Such in-between checks can often be very disrupting to the defense. 19. ... Kc6 20. Rc8+ Kb6 21. Rxc5 Rh7 22. Re5 Kc6 23. Re6+ Kb5 24. Kf5 Rf7+ 25. Rf6 1-0.

95

Rook and Pawn
Position 23
Danny Kopec, 1992
White to move

Category 3: better pawns and king.

White has a dominant king and more space due to the mobile pawns on the queenside. Best is **1. b5!** with the threat 2. Ra3. If 1. ... c6 2. Ke5 is strong. Black's protected passed e-pawn is blockaded.

96

Category 4: better rook and king.

White wins with 1. Kb4 and enters via a5, e.g. **1. Kb4 c5+ 2. Ka5 Rc6 3. e4** (Black will eventually run out of moves). A plan for White to try to force a breakthrough is a3, followed by Rc2 and c4 while Black's rook is tied up.

Rook and Pawn
Position 24
Danny Kopec, 1992
White to move

97

Category 5: better rook.

This is a classic example. White's rook controls the only open file and occupies the seventh rank. One key rule is that you should never exchange a cate-

Rook and Pawn
Position 25
Danny Kopec, 1992
White to move

gory 5 advantage for other advantages unless you are able to calculate a direct win. The point is, once an opponent's rook is active the game can become as unclear as a roulette wheel. Let's explore a model continuation of how White can win from this position.

1. Kf1 Kf8 2. Ke2 Ke8 3. Kd3. First White centralizes his king. **3. ... a6** and Black tries to get some pawns off the seventh to free his rook. **4. f3** White has achieved category 4 (better rook and king).

Should he strive for a completely dominant king, aiming for b6 or d6, or play for the better pawn structure as well, with the possible gain of material? That is a matter of choice. The main thing is never to allow the Black rook to get active for a mere pawn. If White puts his king on b4 Black can keep him out with ... b6, therefore the text continuation. **4. ... b6 5. e4 h6** and if Black takes on e4 White will be able create a passed d-pawn, heading for category 1 (better rook, pawns and king). **6. Ke3** threatening to take on d5, followed by Kf4-e5. **6. ... g5 7. exd5 exd5 8. Rc6 h5 9. Rd6 Rc8 10. Kd2 Rc4 11. Rxd5 f6 12. b3 Rc6 13. h4!,** a little dose of poison. Black has somewhat activated his rook but he'll soon be two pawns down.

98

Rook and Pawn
Position 26
Euwe - Stahlberg
Zurich, 1953
Rook Endings, #276
White to move

Category 2: better pawns.

White wins with **1. Ra4.** Rooks belong behind passed pawns. (Black to move draws with 1. ... Rc1+ 2. Kg2 Ra1 etc.) The White's outside passed a-pawn will decide — even in a king and pawn ending.

99

Rook and Pawn
Position 27
Danny Kopec, 1992
White to move

Category 7: better king.

1. Rc3. After the likely trade of rooks, White's better king ensures victory in the king and pawn ending.

100

Category 4: better rook and king.

37. ... h4. In addition to having the better rook and king, Black now tries this lever to get better pawns. After **38. Rg2 h3 39. Rd2** (39. Rg1 Rf2) **39. ... Rf1** with the idea of ... Rg1-g2.

Rook and Pawn Position 28
J. Finegold - Kopec
World Open, 1975
Black to move

101

Category 2: better rook and pawn.

White wins due to the much better rook and superior pawn structure. White should not chase a pawn while allowing the Black rook to get active. Instead, after **1. Rc6** White should centralize his king.

Rook and Pawn Position 29
Danny Kopec, 1992
White to move

102

Rook and Pawn
Position 30
Danny Kopec, 1992
Black to move

**Category 0:
no advantage.**

1. ... e5 Now Black threatens to play Kf8-e7, driving out White's rook and reaching complete equality, while if 2. Rd8+ Kh7 the Black king can still eventually centralize.

103

Rook and Pawn
Position 31
J. Finegold - Kopec
World Open, 1975
Black to move

**Category 2: better
rook and pawns.**

26. ... Kd6. The Black king tries to aid his rook, and become superior to his counterpart.

104

Category 1: better rook, pawns, and king.

Rook and Pawn Position 32
J. Finegold-Kopec
World Open, 1975

Black to move

27. ... Kc5. The Black king continues his mission to become superior to the White king. Black already has the better rook, and he wants to demonstrate that the White c-pawn is weak, rather than passed and strong. An important point is that 27. ... Kd5? allows 28. Rb2 with counterplay. After 27. ... Kc5, the best try is **28. Rb2 Rb6!** and then 29. Rxb6? Kxb6 reaches a king and pawn ending which is won for Black.

105

Category 3: better pawns & king.

Rook and Pawn Position 33
Danny Kopec, 1992

White to move

White's dominating king and more advanced pawns ensure victory. The winning idea is **c5** and **d6** coupled with **Ra3** (activating the rook).

106

Rook and Pawn
Position 34
Danny Kopec, 1995
White to move

Category 4: better rook and king.

White's rook and king are dramatically superior to Black's. This helps in the subsequent variations where transpositions to king and pawn endings occur.

1. Kb5

Noteworthy in this example is the importance of knowing the subtleties of king and pawn endings as an essential ingredient in the proper conclusion of rook and pawn endings.

1. ... Kf8 2. Ka6 Ke7 3. Kb7 Kd7 4. Rc3!

Threatening Rd3+. (Another way to win is 4. c4. This idea [of a lever] would also have won on White's second move. 4. ... h4 5. f4 Rb8+ 6. Kxb8 Kxc6 and White has a winning king and pawn ending as follows: 7. Kc8 Kd6 [7. ... Kc5 8. Kxc7 Kb4 9. Kxb6 Kxb3 10. c5+-] 8. Kb7 f6 9. g3 hxg3 10. hxg3 f5 11. Kc8 Kc6 12. Kb8 Kd6 [12. ... Kd7 13. c5! would be similar to the main line] 13. Kb7 Kd7 14. c5! bxc5 15. Ka6 Kc6 [15. ... c4 16. bxc4 Kc6 17. Kxa5 is also similar to the main line] 16. Kxa5 c4 17. bxc4 Kc5 18. Ka6 Kxc4 19. Kb7 Kb4 [19. ... c5 20. a5 Kb5 21. a6] 20. Kxc7 Kxa4 21. Kd6 Kb5 22. Ke6 Kc5 23. Kf6 Kd5 24. Kxg6 Ke6 25. Kg5+-; Yet another path to victory at move four would be: 4. Rf6 Rf8 5. f4 Ke7 6. Rc6.)

107

Category 5: better rook.

The Black rook is tied to the defense of his a-pawn and therefore passive. White can use this important factor to improve his position and obtain the better king and better

Rook and Pawn
Position 35
Danny Kopec, 1995
White to move

pawns. Most accurate is **1. Kg4**, followed by h5 and f4. If White plays simply, 1. f4, e.g. 1. ... exf4 2. gxf4 Re8 3. e5 etc., with similar consequences; however, Black can also play 2. ... Rd8! with counterplay. 1. h5, which looks good at first, would allow 1. ... Ra7 followed by 2. ... g6, when White would still have to play Kg4 and f4 to win. So 1. Kg4 is most accurate in terms of order and effect.

Chapter 4

The Other Endings Test

Discussion: The Other Endings Test

Now that we have covered rook and pawn endings it seems natural to round out our effort with other endings. That is what this Test Set is about. It explores diverse material situations where generally one side has an advantage or whereby the defending side is hard-pressed to find the correct drawing move. Some of the many typical material situations covered include: bishop endings, knight endings, bishop vs. knight, bishops of opposite color endings, two bishops vs. bishop and knight, rook and bishop vs. rook and knight, rook vs. knight and bishop, and queen endings. In most instances we have tried to select positions which illustrate the most important concepts related to the ending being tested. Regardless of what you knew before you took this test, we are certain that you will be more knowledgeable about diverse endings when you have completed this test.

Instructions for taking this test

You are allowed two minutes for each of the following positions. Once again, we allow up to four choices for each position. If you find the correct move on your first choice you get one (1) full point, if you find it on your second choice you receive ½-point credit, if you find it on your third choice you receive ⅓-point credit, and a correct move on your fourth choice receives ¼-point credit. You get full credit for the level of difficulty number if any of your four choices are correct. Good luck!

Answer Sheet for Other Endings Test

Position Number	Preferred Choice	2nd Choice	3rd Choice	4th Choice	Side to Move
1.					White
2.					White
3.					Black
4.					White
5.					White
6.					White
7.					Black
8.					Black
9.					Black
10.					White
11.					Black
12.					White
13.					Black
14.					White
15.					Black
16.					White
17.					White
18.					White
19.					White
20.					White
21.					White
22.					White
23.					Black
24.					Black
25.					Black
26.					White
27.					White

108

Other Endings Position 1
White to move

109

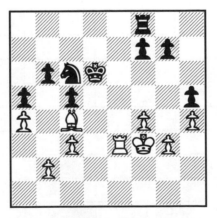

Other Endings Position 2
White to move

110

Other Endings Position 3
Black to move

111

Other Endings Position 4
White to move

112

Other Endings Position 5
White to move

113

Other Endings Position 6
White to move

114

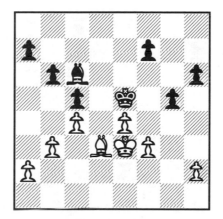

Other Endings Position 7
Black to move

115

Other Endings Position 8
Black to move

116

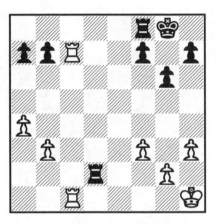

Other Endings Position 9
Black to move

117

Other Endings Position 10
White to move

118

Other Endings Position 11
Black to move

119

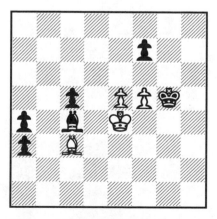

Other Endings Position 12
White to move

120

Other Endings Position 13
Black to move

121

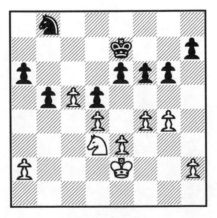

Other Endings Position 14
White to move

122

Other Endings Position 15
Black to move

123

Other Endings Position 16
White to move

124

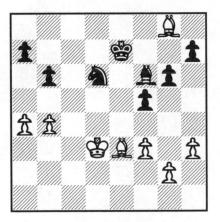

Other Endings Position 17
White to move

125

Other Endings Position 18
White to move

126

Other Endings Position 19
White to move

127

Other Endings Position 20
White to move

128

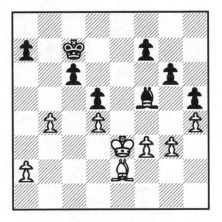

Other Endings Position 21
White to move

129

Other Endings Position 22
White to move

130

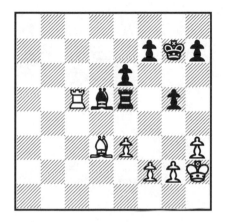

Other Endings Position 23
Black to move

131

Other Endings Position 24
Black to move

132

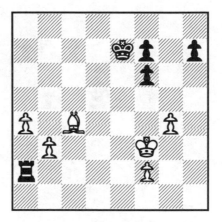

Other Endings Position 25
Black to move

133

Other Endings Position 26
White to move

134

Other Endings Position 27
White to move

Solution Key to Other Endings Test

Position Number	Side to Move	Level of Difficulty	Solution
1.	W	3	1. Bb1
2.	W	2	1. Rd3 +
3.	B	2	1. ... Kc7
4.	W	2	1. b5
5.	W	2	1. Be8
6.	W	3	1. e5
7.	B	2	1. ... Bd7
8.	B	4	1. ... Nc6 +
9.	B	1	1. ... Re8
10.	W	2	1. h4
11.	B	2	1. ... Ke8
12.	W	2	1. e6
13.	B	2	1. ... Kf6
14.	W	2	1. f5
15.	B	2	1. ... Bb3
16.	W	3	1. Kf6
17.	W	2	1. a5
18.	W	2	1. Kh6
19.	W	2	1. Nb3
20.	W	2	1. b3
21.	W	3	1. g4
22.	W	2	1. e5
23.	B	3	1. ... h6
24.	B	2	1. ... Rb1
25.	B	2	1. ... f5
26.	W	2	1. Qf5 +
27.	W	2	1. Bg5

Max = 60

Complete Solutions to Other Endings Test

108

Two bishops vs bishop and knight **48. Bb1!** In *Basic Chess Endings*, Finc explains a step-by-step process whereby the side with the two bishops makes steady progress towards victory. One of the critical components of this process is to drive the defending

Other Endings
Position 1
Two Bishops vs
Bishop
and Knight
Kopec - D. Shapiro
Continental Open,
1976
White to move

king out of the center. That is exactly what the text move accomplishes. From here on, Black gets pushed back, White probes for weaknesses using the long-range "telepower" (Kmoch's term for long-range attacking potential) of the bishops, and wins material. **48. ... Be5 49. Kd3 Bf6 50. b4 Ke6 51. Ba2+ Ke7.** (See test position 17, diagram 124, in this test.) White doesn't win material yet, but he has completed the first three stages of Fine's four stage process (*Basic Chess ESndings*, #267, page 256.) for winning the ending two bishops versus bishop and knight, namely: 1) the Black king has been driven out of the center. 2) the White King's position has been improved and 3) White's bishops have become active.

109

Other Endings
Position 2 Rook and
Bishop vs Rook
and Knight
Fischer - Taimanov
Vancouver, 1971
White to move

36. Rd3+ This move is part of the process by which Fischer will try to demonstrate the superiority of his rook and bishop over Taimanov's rook and knight. The intent of this check is to follow with 37. Rd5 hitting at Black's unprotected h-pawn. Then on 37. ... g6 White's light-squared bishop will have more targets. Instead Taimanov played 37. ... f5 which gave Fischer other light-square weaknesses to focus on.

110

Other Endings
Position 3
Rook and Bishop vs
Rook and Knight
Fischer - Taimanov
Vancouver, 1971
Black to move

Correct was **42. ... Kc7 43. Rd3 Re6+ 44.Kd2 Re8** when Black avoids the trade of rooks. Although White is still winning, Black puts up much stiffer resistance. 42. ... Kd8? is the move played by Taimanov. It allows Fischer to trade into a simpler ending, namely bishop vs. knight, in which he will be able to force a *zugzwang* position.

111

1. b5 This move achieves the most important goal of all queen and pawn endings: a passed pawn which can be escorted by the queen. Of course if White plays 1. Qxc6, Black draws with Qf4+. The game continued: **1. ... cxb5 2. c6 Qc2 3. Qd5** (simpler

Other Endings
Position 4
Queen and Pawn
Ending
*Maroczy -
Bogoljubow*
Dresden, 1936
*Queen and Pawn
Endings,* #214
White to move

was 3. c7 immediately) **3. ... Kh6 4. Qd6 Qc4 5. c7 Kh7 6. Qd7 Qf4+ 7. Kg1 Qc1+ 8. Kf2 Qc5+ 9. Ke2 Qc2+ 10. Ke3 Qc5+ 11. Ke4 Qc4+ 12. Ke5 Qc3+ 13. Kd5 Qc4+ 14. Kd6 Qb4+ 15. Kc6 Qc3+ 16. Kb7+-**. Many people fear and overrate the difficulty of queen endings because of all the checks involved. In practice they are not so hard to calculate.

112

1. Be8 is the winning idea. Fischer effects a *zugzwang* which enables him to sacrifice his bishop for three pawns, allowing the entry of his king. The game ended: **1. ... Kd8**

Other Endings
Position 5
Bishop vs Knight
Fischer - Taimanov
Vancouver, 1971
White to move

2. Bxg6! Nxg6 3. Kxb6 Kd7 4. Kxc5 Ne7 5. b4 axb4 6. cxb4 Nc8 7. a5 Nd6 8. b5 Ne4+ 9. Kb6 Kc8 10. Kc6 Kb8 and Black resigned.

113

Other Endings
Position 6
Exchange Up
Voronkov - Ignatiev
Moscow, 1958
*Rook v. Minor Piece
Endings,* #160
White to move

Here is a situation whereby Black has full material compensation (two pawns) for the exchange, but White has a passed e-pawn which can be used immediately to produce decisive results:

1. e5 g5 2. Rh8 h4 3. Rh7+ Ke6 4. Ke4 Bc5 5. Rh6+ Kd7 6. e6+ Kd8 7. Rh8+ Kc7 8. Rh7+ Kd8 9. Rxb7 g4 10. Rd7+ Ke8 11. Rh7 Bf2 12. Kf4 g3 13. Kf3 h3 14. Rxh3 Ke7 15. Rh6 Kd6 16. Rg6 Be1 17. Kf4! Bf2 18. Kf5 Ke7 19. Rg7+ Ke8 20. Ke5 Be1 21. Kd5 Bf2 22. Kd6 Kf8 23. Rg4. 1-0.

Note how carefully White advanced his passed pawn while making sure that Black's passed pawns were restricted.

114

Other Endings
Position 7
Same Color Bishop Ending
Bonner - Kopec
Richardson Cup, 1981
Black to move

The game position was adjudicated a win for Black. It was the decisive game in the Finals of the Richardson Cup Team Championships of Scotland in 1981. The point is that White has all the inferior features in the position: a worse pawn structure (three islands with pawns fixed on the color of his bishop), the worse king, and the worse bishop (no Black pawns to attack). The winning plan is for Black to put his bishop on e6 or g6 and then to play ... f5. If White takes then after the trade of bishops (otherwise

Black plays Bb1) the ensuing king and pawn ending is lost for White since Black has more tempi thanks to his healthy kingside pawns versus White's split pawns. The White king would have to retreat. If White does not capture on f5 then Black captures on e4. Then if White recaptures with the f-pawn, Black wins with an outside passed g-pawn which is used for decoy while Black wins the e-pawn and the race to the queenside. If White recaptures with bishop, then Black offers a trade with Bf5 leading to a won king and pawn ending. An important move for Black to insert in the whole process is ... a5.

1. ... Bd7 when a sample line might go:

2. Bf1 f5 3. Bd3 fxe4 4. Bxe4 Bf5 5. Bxf5 Kxf5 6. Ke2 a5 7. Ke3 h5 8. Ke2 Kf4 9. Kf2 a4 10. Ke2 g4 11. fxg4 Kxg4 12. Kf2 h4 13. Kg2 h3+ 14. Kf2 Kf4 15. Ke2 Ke4 16. Kf2

16. Kd2 Kf3 17. Kd3 Kg2 18. Ke3 Kxh2 19. Kf2 a3!-+

16. ... Kd3 17. Kg3 a3 18. Kxh3 Kc2 19. Kg4 Kb2 20. h4 Kxa2 21. h5 Kxb3 22. h6 a2 23. h7 a1Q-+.

115

1. ... Nc6+ The only drawing move. After 1. ... Nf3+? 2. Ke3 Ne5 (*2. ... Ne1? 3. Rg1+-*) 3. Rg5! (the only winning move) 3. ... Nc4+ 4. Kd3 Nb2+ 5. Kc3 Na4+ 6. Kb3 Nb6 and

**Other Endings
Position 8
Rook vs Knight
without pawns
Danny Kopec, 1978**
Black to move

now Black's knight is truly stranded. With the help of Ken Thompson's database we know that after 3. Rg5! Black was lost in ten moves. **2. Kd5 Nb4+ 3. Kc4 Nc2=** when the Black king and Black knight are safely together. This position is significant in our studies of king and rook vs. king and knight because it is the first position found where the drawing move for the knight's side had to be a move where Black king and Black knight were further separated, instead of being kept close together as theory recommends.

116

Other Endings
Position 9
Double Rook Ending
Danny Kopec and
Hal Terrie, 1995
Black to move.

1. ... Re8! The rule in rook and pawn endings, and especially endings with four rooks, is that the rooks must be active and preferably connected. Black's rook tries to join its colleague on the second rank. **1. ... Rb8?** loses to 2. Re7 with the idea of Rcc7. Now on: **2. Rxb7 Ree2 3. Rg1 Rb2 4. b4 a5 5. b5 Rb4=** Anytime White may try to activate his king rook Black will respond by doubling on the second (his seventh) rank.

117

Other Endings
Position 10
Knight vs Bad Bishop
Zubareff - Alexandrov
Moscow, 1915
Basic Chess Endings, #251
White to move

1. h4! This is the case of the good knight against the bad bishop. Black's bishop has little to attack and his pawns are fixed on its color. White forces access to the f4-square for his knight from which he will be able to attack Black's two weak points simultaneously: h5 and e6. Black will soon run into *zugzwang* when the White king can force his entry into the Black position. A sequence could go **1. ... gxh4 2. gxh4 Be4** to prevent Ng2. **3. a3** (pass) [3. Nf1 with the idea 4.Nd2 - b3 (or f3) - d4 also wins] **3. ... Bf3 4. Nc2!** followed by Nb4 and wins.

118

The only thing that is important to know in this ending is that the defending king should head for the corner opposite-colored from the bishop. **1. ... Ke8** (1. ... Kc8? 2. Rc1+! Kd8 [2. ... Kb8 3. Rb1+-] 3. Rb1+-)

Other Endings
Position 11
Rook vs Bishop without Pawns
Danny Kopec, 1995

Black to move

119

There are two ideas embedded in this position: (i) White should exchange off all the kingside pawns, even if it costs him his last pawn; and (ii) Black has no way to win with his three queenside pawns because he is left with a passed RP and a bishop of the wrong color. **1. e6 fxe6 2. fxe6 Bxe6 3. Ke5 Bb3 4. Kd6 c4 5. Kc5 Kf5 6. Kb4 a2 7. Ka3 Ke4 8. Kb2 Kd3 9. Ka1!=** In addition, White has a stalemate trick.

Other Endings
Position 12
Bishops of Opposite Color
Maroczy - Pillsbury
Munich, 1900
600 Endings, #227
White to move

120

Other Endings
Position 13
King and Pawn Ending
Cohn - Rubinstein
St. Petersburg, 1909
Black to move

1. ... Kf6! Black is winning this king and pawn ending because White's pawns are weakened in three ways: (i) he has three islands; (ii) he has doubled f-pawns; and (iii) he has fewer pawn tempi available due both to his pawn weaknesses and his pawn advances on the queenside. **2. Kd2 Kg5 3. Ke2 Kh4 4. Kf1 Kh3 5. Kg1 e5!** and now White's lack of pawn moves becomes evident. **6. Kh1 b5 7. Kg1 f5 8. Kh1 g5 9. Kg1 h5 10. Kh1 g4 11. e4 fxe4 12. fxe4 h4 13. Kg1 g3 14. hxg3 hxg3 0-1.**

121

Other Endings Position 14
Knight and Pawn Ending
Pillsbury - Gunsberg
Hastings, 1895
Basic Chess Endings, #135
White to move

1. f5! This position is noteworthy because the most basic elements of pawn structure prevail, notwithstanding the presence of knights. The text is a fundamental lever which strikes at the heart of Black's position. **1. ... g5 2. Nb4!! a5 3. c6!! Kd6 4. fxe6!! Nxc6** (4. ... axb4 5. e7 Kxe7 6. c7+-) **5. Nxc6 Kxc6 6. e4+-.** Connected passed pawns nearly always win.

122

This position illustrates the main aspect of bishops of opposite- color endings: Block your opponent's pawns on the color of his bishop, while advancing your pawns through the color of the opposing bishop whenever feasible.

Other Endings
Position 15
Bishops of Opposite Color
Berger - Mackenzie
Frankfurt, 1887
Basic Chess Endings, #210
Black to move

1. ... Bb3 2. Bb8 a5! 3. Bc7 a4 4. Bxb6 a3 5. d5 Bxd5 (5. ... Bc4? 6. d6 a2 7. d7 a1Q+ 8. Kh2=) **6. Bd4+ f6 7. c4 Bxc4 8. Kf2 Kf7 9. Ke3 Ke6 10. g3 g5 11. h4 gxh4 12. gxh4 f5**, and the widely separated passed pawns win for Black (a second important concept for winning bishop of opposite color endings).

123

A remarkably poignant position considering the reduced material.

Other Endings
Position 16
King and Pawn Ending
Bogoljubow - Selezniev
Moravska Ostravo, 1923
600 Endings, #116
White to move

1. Kf6 Ke8 2. Kg7 Ke7 3. g3! Ke6 4. Kf8 Kf6 5. g4 Ke6 6. g5 f5 (6. ... f6 7. h5!!) **7. h5 f4 8. hxg6+-.**

124

Other Endings Position 17
Two Bishops vs Bishop
and Knight
Kopec - Shapiro (2)
Continental Open, 1976
White to move

The continuation from the earlier Kopec-Shapiro game fragment. Now that White has achieved activity for his bishops and king, it is important to probe Black's position further. **54. a5!** This move forces the necessary opening of further avenues to Black's position, not 54. Bxh7? Kf7 trapping the bishop. Instead White holds that threat in reserve.

125

Other Endings
Position 18
King and Pawn Ending
Mastering Chess, p. 89
White to move

1. Kh6 Kg8 2. h4! And it is clear that the lever h5 will win for White.

126

As *Mastering Chess* Co-author Ian Mullen suggests: Alekhine's winning plan is to convert his spatial advantage and better knight into the advantage

Other Endings
Position 19
Knight and Pawn Ending
Alekhine - Anderson
Mastering Chess, p. 94
White to move

of an outside passed pawn by trading his d-pawn for one of Black's queenside pawns. **1. Nb3! Kf8** (1. ... Ne7 2. Na5 Nxd5 3. Nxb7 Nb4 4. Nxd6 Nd3+ *[4. ... Nxa2+ 5. Kc2 Nb4+ 6. Kc3 and the White king enters quickly.]* 5. Kc2 Nxf2 6. b4! Kf8 7. b5+-) **2. Na5 b6 3. Nc6 Ke8 4. Kd2 Ne7 5. Nxa7 Nxd5 6. Nb5 Kd7 7. Nd4 g6 8. a4 Nc7 9. Kc3 g5 10. Kb4 d5 11. Nf3 f6 12. Nd4 Kd6?** (loses quickly) (12. ... Ke7 13. a5 bxa5+ 14. Kxa5 Kd7 15. b4 Kc8 16. Kb6+-) **13. Nb5+ Nxb5 14. Kxb5 Ke5 15. b4 d4 16. Kc4+-.**

127

1. b3 and Black is in *zugzwang*! On any knight move Bb4+ follows on 1. ... Kc6 2. Ke5 Kc5 3. Bc1!. (3. Ke6 does not win because of 3. ... Kd4 4. Kf7 Kd3 5. Kxg6 Kxd2 6.

Other Endings
Position 20
Bishop vs Knight
Flohr - Levenfish
Leningrad vs. Moscow, 1939
Basic Chess Endings, #241
White to move

Kxf5 Kc2). And White will make slow but steady progress to victory.

128

Other Endings Position 21
Same Color Bishops
Portisch - Reshevsky
Palma de Mallorca, 1970
600 Endings #218
White to move

Portisch demonstrates the significance of the fact that Black's pawns are fixed on light squares. In all variations White forces an outside passed h-pawn. **1. g4 Bb1** (1. ... hxg4 2. fxg4 Bb1 when White's outside passed h-pawn will win easily.) **2. gxh5 gxh5 3. f4 Kd6** (3. ... Bxa2 4. Bxh5 f6 5. Bg6 Kd6 6. h5 Ke7 7. h6 Kf8 8. Kf3+-) **4. Bxh5 Ke7 5. a3 Bf5 6. Kf3 Bd7 7. Kg3 Kf8 8. Bg4 f5 9. Be2 Kg7 10. h5 Kh6 11. Kh4 Be8 12. Bd3 Bd7 13. Ba6 Be6 14. Bb7 Bd7 15. a4** (*Zugzwang!*) **15. ... Be8 16. Bc8 Bxh5 17. Bd7 Bd1 18. Bxc6 Kg6 19. a5 Kf6 20. b5.**

129

Other Endings Position 22
Queen and Knight vs
Queen and Bishop
Jansa - Hennings
Karlovi Vari, 1973
The Best Move,
diagram #212
White to move

It is generally accepted that the knight and queen coordinate better than the bishop and queen. In the diagrammed position the dark squares around the Black king are weakened. This offers an ideal opportunity for the White knight and White queen to attempt to infiltrate this board sector. In addition the Black queenside pawns and his passed queen pawn are somewhat disjointed. The knight is an ideal piece for blockading and destroying such weakened formations. **1. e5 Qd8 2. Ne4!** (threatening Qh6) **2. ... Kh7** (2. ... Kg7 3. Nd6 Bd5 4. Qxd4 Qg5 5. f3 h4 6. e6+ Kh7 [6. ... Kf8 7. Qh8+ Ke7 8. Qd8+!; 6. ... f6 7. Qa7+ Kg8 8. Qb8+ Kh7 9. Ne8] 7. Qh8+!) **3. Nd6 Bd5 4. Nxf7 Qf8 5. Ng5+ Kg7 6. Qxd4** and White wins.

130

This is a noteworthy position for its apparent simplicity and the likelihood that a player with the Black position would underestimate the dangers confronting him.

Other Endings
Position 23
Rook and Bishop vs Rook and Bishop (same color)
Forintos - Jansa
Vrnjacka Banja, 1973
The Best Move,
diagram #216
Black to move

1. ... h6 If instead 1. ... f5? 2. g4! The main idea behind this move is to undermine the protection of Black's bishop. *(White threatens 3. gxf5 exf5 4. Bc4 winning. If Black now plays 2. ... fxg4?, White has 3. e4 winning.)* 2. ... Kf6 3. gxf5 exf5 *(3. ... h6 4. fxe6 Kxe6 5. Kg3 Kd6 6. Ra5 with a winning ending)* 4. f4! wins a piece. The try 1. ... Kf6 just loses a pawn to Bxh7. **2. e4 Bxe4 3. Rxe5 Bxd3** when according to Hort and Jansa "Black has a pawn for the exchange and with all the pawns on the same flank the position is an easy draw."

131

In endings involving rooks, the single most important factor is the activity of the rooks involved. Here Black has a rook against a bishop and knight. He needs to win a

Other Endings
Position 24
Rook vs Two Minor Pieces
Reti - Bogolubov
Bad Kissingen, 1928
Basic Chess Endings, #452
Black to move

pawn or two as further compensation for his material deficit. Therefore the correct move is:

1. ... Rb1 Black threatens ... Rxb3 as well as ... Rb2. **2. Ne3 Rxb3 3. a5 b5 4. axb6 Rxb6** Now the game should have continued: **5 Nc4** (Instead play continued: 5. Ke2? Rb4! 6. Kf3 Kf7 7. Bh4 Rb1

8. Nc4 Ke6 9. Bg3 Rc1 10. Na5 *[10. Nxe5? Rc3+ 11. Kf2 Rxg3-+]*
10. ... Ra1 11. Nc4 Ra4 12. Ne3 a5 13. Be1 Ra3 14. Ke2 a4 15. Nc2
Rb3 16. Bb4 and Black eventually won this ending which should
have been drawn.) **5. ... Rb4 6. Nxe5 Rxe4 7. Nc6 Kf7 8. Be3 Ke6
9. Ke2 Kd5 10. Na5 Ra4 11. Bd2 Kc5 12. Kd3 Kb5 13. Nb7** And
according to Fine "since the Black rook pawn still cannot advance
a draw must result."

132

Other Endings Position 25
Exchange Up
Spassky - Fischer #21
Match 1972
Black to move

This is the last
game of the famous
1972 "Match of the
Century" between
Boris Spassky and
Bobby Fischer.
Fischer (Black) has
been the exchange
up for many moves and is looking for a way to convert his slight
material advantage (technically speaking White only has one
pawn for the exchange) and Spassky has just given him this
opportunity by playing 30. g4?. The reason this move is bad is
because it allows Black to undouble his f-pawns and force an outside passed h-pawn. It is also noteworthy that White's ever-dan-
gerous connected passed pawns on the queenside have been fully contained by Black's rook: **30. ... f5 31. gxf5** (31. g5 f6-+) **31. ...
f6 32. Bg8 h6 33. Kg3 Kd6 34. Kf3 Ra1 35. Kg2 Ke5 36. Be6 Kf4
37. Bd7 Rb1 38. Be6 Rb2 39. Bc4 Ra2 40. Be6 h5 41. Bd7.** The
game was adjourned here but Spassky resigned without further
play. **0-1**

133

1. Qf5+ Now both ... Ke8 and ... Ke7 lose to 2. Qf7+. (1. Qd5?! Qa4+ 2. Kb1 Ke7 and White still has to work to win.)

Other Endings
Position 26
Queen and Pawn Ending
Kopec - J. Fang
Monadnock Marathon, 1991
White to move

1. ... Kg8 2. Qd5
Qb5? and White wins the K+P ending.(2. ... Kh7 3. Qe4+ Kg8 4. e7 Qa4+ 5. Kb1 Qe8 6. Qxc4+).

134

1. Bg5 This move is so strong in demonstrating the power of two bishops, and the helplessness of two knights when passively posted and required to defend each

Other Endings
Position 27
Two Bishops vs Two Knights
Botvinnik - Bronstein
World Championship, 1951
600 Endings, #262
White to move

other, that Black resigned. A possible continuation might have been: **1. ... Nc6 2. Bxd5 Nd6 3. Bf3** when White's passed d-pawn and Black's weak pawns ensure White's victory.

Chapter 5

The Novice Test

Instructions for taking this test

You are allowed two minutes for each of the positions in this test. In each position, select the one move you think is best. In some positions, more than one move will be accepted as correct. Your score will be based on the total number correct. A full discussion of the scoring is at the end of the test.

Answer Sheet for Novice Test

Position Number	Best Move	Side to Move
1.		White
2.		White
3.		White
4.		White
5.		Black
6.		White
7.		Black
8.		White
9.		White
10.		White
11.		White
12.		White
13.		Black
14.		White
15.		White
16.		Black
17.		White
18.		White
19.		White
20.		Black
21.		White
22.		Black
23.		Black
24.		Black

135

Novtest Position 1
White to move

136

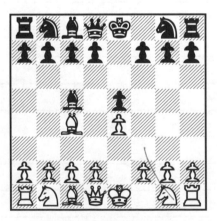

Novtest Position 2
White to move

137

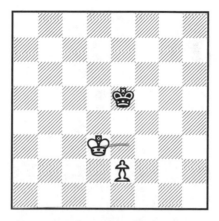

Novtest Position 3
White to move

138

Novtest Position 4
White to move

139

Novtest Position 5
Black to move

140

Novtest Position 6
White to move

141

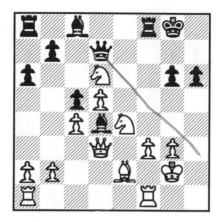

Novtest Position 7
Black to move

142

Novtest Position 8
White to move

143

Novtest Position 9
White to move

144

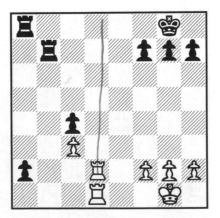

Novtest Position 10
White to move

145

Novtest Position 11
White to move

146

Novtest Position 12
White to move

147

Novtest Position 13
Black to move

148

Novtest Position 14
White to move

149

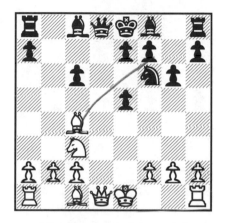

Novtest Position 15
White to move

150

Novtest Position 16
Black to move

151

Novtest Position 17
White to move

152

Novtest Position 18
White to move

153

Novtest Position 19
White to move

154

Novtest Position 20
Black to move

155

Novtest Position 21
White to move

156

Novtest Position 22
Black to move

157

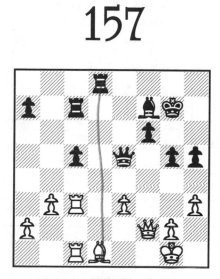

Novtest Position 23
Black to move

158

Novtest Position 24
Black to move

Solution Key to Novice Test

Position Number	Side to Move	Phase of Game	Level of Difficulty	Solution
1.	W	M	1	1. Rh7 +
2.	W	O	1	1. Nf3, 1. Nc3, 1. d3
3.	W	E	3	1. Ke3
4.	W	O	1	1. 0-0,1. d3
5.	B	M	3	1. ... Rg1 +
6.	W	E	2	1. Bxd6
7.	B	M	1	1. ... Qh3#
8.	W	O	3	1. e3, 1. Nf3, 1. Qc2, 1. Rc1
9.	W	E	2	1. Rd1
10.	W	M	1	1. Rd8 +
11.	W	O	3	1. Bxf6
12.	W	M	2	1. f6
13.	B	O	1	1. ... bxc6
14.	W	E	3	1. g5
15	W	O	1	1. Bxf7 +
16.	B	M	3	1. ... Ra1 +
17.	W	E	2	1. g4
18.	W	O	2	1. Bxc6
19.	W	E	1	1. Rc1, 1. Ra1
20.	B	M	2	1. ... f4
21.	W	O	1	1. Bd3, 1. Nc3
22.	B	E	2	1. ... Rb2
23.	B	M	3	1. ... Rxd1 +
24.	B	E	3	1. ... Nf4

Max = 47

Discussion and Scoring: The Novice Test

As mentioned in the general introduction, the Novice test was developed by Hal Terrie for the Kopec Chess Camp, to test players whom we felt, based on previous experience, were not strong enough to benefit from the Tests in Chapter 1 and 2. Since 1995, the test has been administered to hundreds of campers. The results have confirmed the correlation between score and rating proposed at that time:

Score	Rating
21-24	1500 or higher
18-20	1300-1500
14-17	1200-1300
11-13	1100 -1200
7- 10	1000-1100
under 7	under 1000

You can evaluate your performance on the test not only from the total number correct but also based on phase of the game and difficulty of the positions. There are eight positions each in the opening, middlegame and endgame. The positions are also assigned a level of difficulty, from one (easiest) to three (hardest). Thus, for instance, doing well on level-three middlegames but poorly on level two and three endings would mean that tactics are good but you lack essential endgame knowledge; a reverse performance would mean tactics are weak and need study. And so on. In addition there is feedback in the solutions section on the type of chess theme or knowledge being tested.

Complete Solutions to the Novice Test

135

Novtest Position 1
Skewer Wins Queen

Comprehensive Chess Course, Vol. II, #375
(modified)
White to move

1. Rh7+ Bxh7 2. Rxh7+ +-.

136

Novtest Position 2
Development

White to move

(1. e4 e5 2. Bc4 Bc5) Acceptable moves: **3. Nf3**, **3. Nc3**, **3. d3** but not 3. Qf3 or 3. Qh5. It is important to develop the minor pieces first, before considering queen moves. The move 3. Qe2 is a decent move, known to theory. However, it is not accepted here as a correct answer because this test is for novice players, who should be discouraged from making early queen moves.

137

1. Ke3 The only way to win. In order to win an ending with king and one pawn vs king, the superior side must (1) be in front of the pawn and (2) have the opposition.

Novtest Position 3
Opposition
White to move

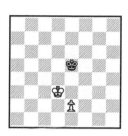

138

(1. e4 e5 2. Nf3 Nc6 3. Nc3 Nf6 4. Bc4 Bc5) Acceptable moves: **5. d3, 5. 0-0** but not 5. Ng5, which would be a wasted move after the normal develop-

Novtest Position 4
Development
White to move

ing move 5. ... 0-0, when it would be very bad to consider trading two pieces for rook and pawn with knight (or bishop) xf7.

139

1. ... Rg1+! 2. Kxg1 Nxe2-+ knight fork. No credit for 1. ... Rg2 or 1. ... Nh3, which are good moves but not nearly as efficient as 1. ... Rg1+.

Novtest Position 5
Knight Fork
Comprehensive Chess Course, (modified)
Black to move

140

Novtest Position 6
Simplify When Ahead
Hal Terrie, 1995
White to move

1. Bxd6. If White tries 1. Kd4? instead, then 1. ... Nc4 gives him real trouble. When ahead material in the endgame, always aim for the simplest available position by exchanging the defending pieces.

141

Novtest Position 7
Mate in One
Bobby Fischer Teaches Chess, #44
Black to move

1. ... Qh3#.

142

Novtest Position 8
Development/
Calculation
White to move

(1. d4 d5 2. c4 e6 3. Nc3 Nf6 4. Bg5 Nbd7 5. cxd5 exd5) Acceptable moves: **6. e3, 6. Nf3, 6. Qc2, 6. Rc1.** Not 6. Nxd5?? Nxd5! 7. Bxd8 Bb4+ 8. Qd2 Bxd2+ 9. Kxd2 Kxd8 with a piece up.

143

1. Rd1 (1. Re1? allows Black to prevent White's rook from reaching the 7th rank by ... Kf8) **1. ... Kf8 2. Rd7±.**

Novtest Position 9
Seventh Rank
Hal Terrie, 1995
White to move

144

1. Rd8+ Rxd8 2. Rxd8#. Modification of Fischer, p. 112 #88. 1-0

Novtest Position 10
Back Rank
Bobby Fischer Teaches Chess, #88 (modified)
White to move

145

(1. e4 e5 2. Nf3 Nc6 3. Bb5 Bc5 4. 0-0 Nd4 5. Nxd4 Bxd4 6. c3 Bb6 7. d3 c6 8. Bc4 Nf6 9. Bg5 d6 10. Kh1 Bg4) White wins a piece: **11. Bxf6 Bxd1** (11. ... Qxf6 12. Qxg4+-) **12. Bxd8 Be2** (12. ... Rxd8 13. Rxd1+-) **13. Re1 Bxd3 14. Bxd3 Rxd8** and White is a piece up.

Novtest Position 11
Tactic Wins Piece
White to move

146

Novtest Position 12
Sweeper/Clearance
Hal Terrie, 1995

White to move

1. f6! 1. Nh5 is not forceful enough — Black responds with 1. ... Qh4! and has chances to defend himself. **1. ... gxf6** (1. ... Qd7 2. fxg7+-) **2. Nf5+-.**

147

Novtest Position 13
Only One Recapture

Black to move

(1. e4 c5 2. Nf3 d6 3. d4 cxd4 4. Nxd4 Nf6 5. Nc3 Nc6 6. Bc4 Qb6 7. Nxc6) Acceptable move: **7. ... bxc6** but not 7. ... Qxc6?? 8. Bb5.

148

Novtest Position 14
Pawn
Tempo/Opposition
Hal Terrie, 1995

White to move

1. g5, taking the opposition. The move 1. Kd4 does not throw away the win but does not make progress either, as White will have to play g5 soon anyway. 1. f5+? only draws, as after 1. ... gxf5 2. gxf5+ Kf6 White does not fulfill the necessary conditions for a king and pawn vs king win: He is not in front of his pawn and does not have opposition.

149

(1. e4 c5 2. Nf3 d6 3. d4 cxd4 4. Nxd4 Nf6 5. Nc3 Nc6 6. Bc4 g6? 7. Nxc6 bxc6 8. e5 dxe5??) Now **9. Bxf7+** wins the queen.

Novtest Position 15
Tactic Wins Queen
White to move

150

1. ... Ra1+
2. Nxa1 Qa2#.

Novtest Position 16
Clearance
Winning Chess Tactics for Juniors, #283
Black to move

151

1. g4 Once again, White uses a pawn tempo to gain the opposition.

Novtest Position 17
Pawn Tempo/Opposition
Hal Terrie, 1995
White to move

152

Novtest Position 18
Removing Defender
Wins Pawn

White to move

(1. e4 e5 2. Nf3 Nc6 3. Bb5 a6 4. Ba4 Nf6 5. 0-0 Be7 6. Re1 d6 7. d4 0-0) Acceptable move: **8. Bxc6.** This wins a pawn after **8. ... bxc6 9. dxe5 dxe5 10. Qxd8 Rxd8 11. Nxe5.**

153

Novtest Position 19
Queening/Back Rank
Hal Terrie, 1995

White to move

1. Rc1! Or **1. Ra1!**.

154

Novtest Position 20
Lever
Hal Terrie, 1995

Black to move

1. ... f4!, an attacking lever which destroys White's position.

155

(1. e4 c5 2. Nf3 e6 3. d4 cxd4 4. Nxd4 Nf6) Acceptable moves: **5. Nc3, 5. Bd3** but not 5. e5?? Qa5+.

Novtest Position 21
Development/
Calculation
White to move

156

1. ... Rb2= Rooks belong behind passed pawns! If 1. ... Rb8?, then 2. Rb1±.

Novtest Position 22
Rook Behind Passed
Pawn
Hal Terrie, 1995
Black to move

157

1. ... Rxd1+!
2. Rxd1 Qxc3.

Novtest Position 23
Overloaded Piece
*Winning Chess Tactics
for Juniors,* #313
Black to move

158

Novtest Position 24
Knight vs Bad
Bishop/*Zugzwang*
Hal Terrie, 1995
Black to move

1. ... Nf4 (1. ... Ng5 is not as good because after 2. Bf1 Black's best is still to aim the knight at f4, which he could have done on move 1: 2. ... Ne6 [On 2. ... f6 White has 3. *Bg2 Ne6* and once again *4. g5!,* though complicated, gives White good chances to hold.] 3. g5 [3. *Be2 Nf4* transposes to the main line.] 3. ... Nf4 and wins as in the main line. [Not 3. ... *Nxg5 4. Bg2 f6 5. Bf1 Ne6 6. Be2*]; If 1. ...f6 2. g5! fxg5 [2. ... *Nxg5 3. Bg4*] 3. Bg4 Black may still be winning but it will be much harder now. It's important to find the most accurate sequence; if 1. ... Nd4 2. Bd1 f6 3. g5 fxg5 [3. ... *f5? 4. g6*] 4. Bg4.) **2. Bf1 f6 3. Kc2 Kd4 4. Kd2 c5 5. Kc2 Ke3** and wins.

Chapter 6

The Intermediate Test

Instructions for taking this test

You are allowed a total of two minutes for each of the following positions to select your preferred move(s) and to write down as many as four choices in order of preference. Write your first choice in the column labeled "Preferred Move". Write your secondary choices in the columns labeled "2nd Choice", "3rd Choice", "4th Choice". You will receive partial credit for correct move selections in any column. If your first choice is the correct move, you receive one (1) full point credit, if your second choice is correct, 1/2-point credit, if your third choice is correct it gives 1/3-point credit, and a fourth choice correct gives 1/4-point credit.

Answer Sheet for Intermediate Test

Position Number	Preferred Choice	2nd Choice	3rd Choice	4th Choice	Side to Move
1.					White
2.					Black
3.					Black
4.					Black
5.					Black
6.					White
7.					White
8.					White
9.					Black
10.					Black
11.					White
12.					White
13.					Black
14.					White
15.					Black
16.					White
17.					Black
18.					White
19.					White
20.					Black
21.					Black
22.					White
23.					Black
24.					White

159

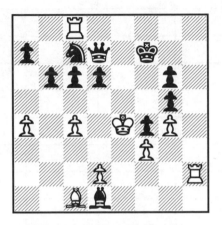

Intermediate Position 1
White to Move

160

Intermediate Position 2
Black to move

161

Intermediate Position 3
Black to move

162

Intermediate Position 4
Black to move

163

Intermediate Position 5
Black to move

164

Intermediate Position 6
White to move

165

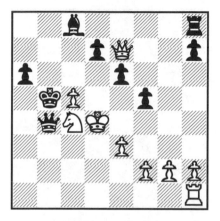

Intermediate Position 7
White to move

166

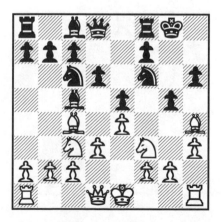

Intermediate Position 8
White to move

167

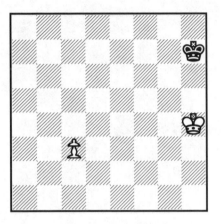

Intermediate Position 9
Black to move

168

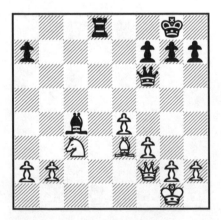

Intermediate Position 10
Black to move

169

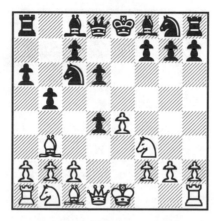

Intermediate Position 11
White to move

170

Intermediate Position 12
White to move

171

Intermediate Position 13
Black to move

172

Intermediate Position 14
White to move

173

Intermediate Position 15
Black to move

174

Intermediate Position 16
White to move

175

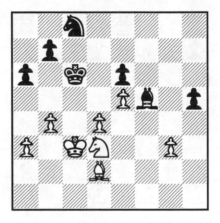

Intermediate Position 17
Black to move

176

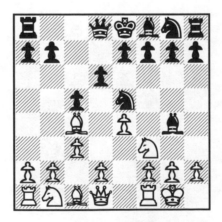

Intermediate Position 18
White to move

177

Intermediate Position 19
White to move

178

Intermediate Position 20
Black to move

179

Intermediate Position 21
Black to move

180

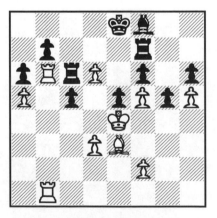

Intermediate Position 22
White to move

181

Intermediate Position 23
Black to move

182

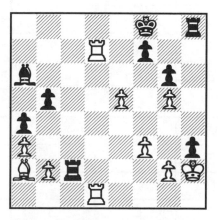

Intermediate Position 24
White to move

Solution Key to Intermediate Test

Position Number	Side to Move	Phase of Game	Level of Difficulty	Solution
1.	W	M	1	1. Rxc7
2.	B	O	2	1. ... Na5
3.	B	E	2	1. ...Rb8, 1. ...Rd8
4.	B	O	1	1. ...Nxb3
5.	B	M	1	1. ... Rxd2
6.	W	E	2	1. b5
7.	W	M	1	1. Rb1
8.	W	O	3	1. Nxg5
9.	B	E	2	1. ... Kh6
10.	B	M	2	1. ... Qxc3
11.	W	O	2	1. Bd5
12.	W	M	3	1. Rf8 +
13.	B	O	3	1. ... Qb4
14.	W	E	1	1. Kd4
15	B	O	1	1. ... Qb6
16.	W	M	3	1. Bxc3
17.	B	E	2	1. ... Bxd3
18.	W	O	2	1. Nxe5
19.	W	E	3	1. Kb1
20.	B	M	3	1. ... Rxe4
21.	B	O	2	1. ... Qd7
22.	W	E	3	1. Rxc6
23.	B	M	2	1. ... Ng5
24.	W	E	3	1. Rd8 +

Max = 50

Discussion and Scoring: The Intermediate Test

After a few years of experience with the Novice Test, we decided that a new test was needed to evaluate those with playing strength between roughly 1500 and 1800. The Intermediate Test, designed in the year 2000, is the result. Experience with this test is still very limited but the results so far (in 2000 and 2001) suggest that it is more difficult than intended, with the upper limit being 1900 or more. A preliminary rating/score equivalence table is given below. When more test scores are available for analysis, we will publish an updated table, perhaps on the Kopec website (www.kopecchess.com).

Score	Rating
19-24	Above 1800
13-18	1650-1800
7-12	1500-1650
under 7	1500 or below

You can evaluate your performance on this test not only from the total number correct but also based on phase of the game and difficulty of the positions. There are eight positions each in the opening, middlegame and endgame. The positions are also assigned a level of difficulty, from one (easiest) to three (hardest). Thus, for instance, doing well on level three middlegames but poorly on level two and three endings would mean that tactics are good but you lack essential endgame knowlege; a reverse performance would mean tactics are weak and need study. And so on.

Complete Solutions for the Intermediate Test

159

Intermediate Position 1

Danny Kopec, 2000
Black to move

Deflection, Skewer

Best is **1. Rxc7** (1. Rh7+ is not as good: 1. ... Ke6 2. Rxd7 Kxd7 3. Rg8 when White has only an extra exchange.) **1. ... Qxc7 2. Rh7+ Ke6 3. Rxc7** when White is ahead a full rook. A lot of time was spent constructing this position to ensure that the tactics actually work out. The main idea is that deeper analysis (of 1. Rxc7) reveals that the text is better than 1. Rh7+?

160

Intermediate Position 2

Ruy Lopez
Cozio Variation
Black to Move

Recognizing Opening Threat

6. ... Na5 is the only move which deals with the dual threats of Qb3 and Ng5. This is an example of recognizing and dealing with threats. In order to progress in chess one must be able to do this.

161

Activate Rook

Black must sacrifice a pawn to activate his rook: **1. ... Rb8** (or ... Rd8 [Not 1. ... Re8? 2. Kf1]) **2. Rxa5 Rb1+ 3. Kg2 Ra1.** With the

Intermediate Position 3

Danny Kopec and Hal Terrie, 2000
Black to move

rook behind the passed pawn, Black can draw. This is an example of the kind of specific endgame knowledge (R+3+a-pawn vs. R+3, rook behind a pawn, [with ... h5] draws) that strong players must have.

162

Accurate Opening Play

This arises after the opening moves 1. e4 e5 2. Nf3 Nc6 3. Bb5 a6 4. Ba4 d6 5. 0-0 b5 6. Bb3 Na5 7. d4. Now **7. ... Nxb3** is probably

Intermediate Position 4

Ruy Lopez
Tournament Variation
Black to move

Black's best since 7. ... exd4 8. Nxd4 and Not 8. Qxd4? c5 9. Qd5 Be6 followed by ... c4. Both sides must be aware of the "Noah's ark Trick" starting with ... c5 and 8. ... c5 9. Bd5 gives White an edge.

163

Intermediate Position 5

Danny Kopec, 2000

Black to move

Undermining Combination

1. ... Rxd2 2. Qxd2 Nxe4 and Black wins two pieces for a rook. This is an example of an undermining combination. It works because the White Queen is overloaded.

164

Intermediate Position 6

Danny Kopec, 2000

White to move

Line Opening Lever

6. 1. b5! White opens a file to activate his rook and exploit the inability of Black's pieces to coordinate. This is an example of a "lever" to open lines. **1. ... cxb5** (If 1. ... Nb8 2. bxc6 Nxc6 [*2. ... bxc6 3. Rb1 Nd7 4. Rb7 Nf6 5. Rb8+ Kh7 6. a4*] 3. Rb1 Nd8 4. Rb5 and again White wins easily.) **2. Rc7 Nb6 3. Rxb7 Nc4 4. Kf2** (More accurate than 4. Ke2 Na3 5. Rd7 Nb1.) **4. ... Na3 5. Rd7 Bg6 6. Rxd5 Kf8** (6. ... Bb1 7. Rd8+ Kh7 8. d5 should win easily enough for White.) **7. Rd7 Ke8 8. Ra7 b4 9. e4.** And again White should have every expectation to win.

165

Decoy, Knight Fork

1. Rb1 Qxb1 2. Na3+.
An example of a
"decoy" sacrifice to
create a fork.

Intermediate
Position 7
Kopec-de Firmian
Thousand Oaks, CA,
1985
White to move

166

Sacrifice to
Exploit Pin

This arises after the
opening moves: 1. e4
e5 2. Nf3 Nc6 3. Bc4
Nf6 4. d3 Bc5 5. Nc3 d6
6. h3 0-0 7. Bg5 h6 8.

Intermediate
Position 8
Danny Kopec and
Hal Terrie, 2000
White to move

Bh4 g5. **9. Nxg5 hxg5 10. Bxg5 Bb4 11. 0-0** (Also 11. Qf3 Kg7 12. Qg3 is interesting.) **11. ... Bxc3 12. bxc3** Black is helpless against the threat of f4. For example: **12. ... Qe7** (Other tries are equally hopeless: 12. ... Na5 13. f4 Nxc4 14. fxe5! [the routine *14. dxc4* also wins, though more slowly: *14. ... Qe7 15. fxe5 Qxe5 16. Bxf6 Qxe4 17. Rf3 Qg6 18. Qd4 Bf5 19. Qh4 Qh7 20. Qg5+ Bg6 21. Rf4*] 14. ... Nxe5 [*14. ... Ne3 15. Qf3*] 15. Bxf6 Qd7 16. Qh5 Ng6 17. Qh6.) **13. f4** (Another way to play it, which also wins, is 13. Qf3 Kg7 14. Qg3 Nh5. There is really no choice about this, as in addition to 15. f4 White also threatens to regain the piece with Bh4+ and Qg5. 15. Bxe7+ Nxg3 16. Bxf8+ Kxf8 17. fxg3+) **13. ... exf4 14. Rxf4** (White can also try 14. d4 threatening simply Rxf4 and Bxf6. Black would have no choice but to return the piece. However, after 14. ... Qxe4 15. Bxf6 Qf5 White must play 16. Bh4 and although material equality has been reestablished, White's advantage is a lot less decisive than the main line, where he remains behind in material and even sacrifices more!)

14. ... Qe5 However, very strong now is h4, e.g. **15. h4! Nh7** (15. ... Ne8 16. Qh5 Be6 17. d4 Qg7 18. Bxe6 fxe6 19. Rg4 White wins [*19. Rxf8+ Kxf8 20. Rf1+ Kg8 21. Bh6 Nf6*]) **16. Qh5 Nxg5 17. hxg5 Qxf4 18. g6** (If 18. Rf1 Qxf1+ 19. Kxf1 Be6 and White has nothing. Note that if 20. Bxe6 fxe6+ is check.) **18. ... Kg7** (18. ... Qe3+ is not as good: 19. Kh1 Kg7 20. Qh7+ Kf6 21. Rf1+ Ke7 22. Rxf7+ Rxf7 23. Qxf7+ Kd8 24. Qf6+ Ne7 25. g7 Qe1+ [*25. ... Qg3*] 26. Kh2+-) **19. Qh7+ Kf6 20. Rf1** (20. g7 looks good at first but after 20. ... Be6 21. gxf8Q Rxf8 22. Rf1 Qxf1+ 23. Kxf1 Bxc4 24. dxc4 Ne5 White might not be able to win despite his material advantage.) **20. ... Qxf1+ 21. Kxf1 Be6** (If 21. ... fxg6 22. Qxc7 and Black will have trouble finishing his development.) **22. Bxe6 Kxe6** (If 22. ... fxe6 23. Qxc7 and once again White is chopping up Black's position. A sample line might be 23. ... Kxg6+ 24. Ke2 Rf7 25. Qxd6 Re8 26. d4 with many unpleasant threats.) **23. g7 Rg8 24. d4 Ke7** (If 24. ... Ne7 25. Qh3+ Kf6 26. Qd7 and once again Black's queenside gets devoured.) **25. e5 dxe5 26. d5 Na5 27. Qf5 Rxg7 28. Qxe5+ Kf8 29. Qxc7 b6 30. d6** and so on. We do not mean to befuddle the reader with variations — but this is a sacrifice which must be played somewhat intuitively. The idea is that the N/f6 lacks protection (from a B/e7) and the pin on f6 is long term and devastating. The variations are given to support our intuition.

167

Intermediate Position 9

Black to move

Opposition

1. ... Kh6 is the only move to draw. Black must take the opposition and yet stay within the square of the pawn.(1. ... Kg6? 2. Kg4 Kf6 3. Kf4 Ke6 4. Ke4 Kd6 5. Kd4 Kc6 6. Kc4 Kb6 7. Kd5+-; 1. ... Kg7? 2. Kg5 also wins for White.)

168

Back Rank Vulnerability

Intermediate Position 10

Black to move

White has two pawns for the exchange so Black must find this tactical opportunity to win. **20. ... Qxc3! 21. bxc3 Rd1+ 22. Qe1** (22. Qf1 Rxf1) **22. ... Rxe1+ 23. Kf2 Re2+** and Black wins.

169

Noah's Ark Trap

Intermediate Position 11

Ruy Lopez

Steinitz Variation

White to move

This arises after the opening moves 1. e4 e5 2. Nf3 Nc6 3. Bb5 a6 4. Ba4 d6 5. d4 b5 6. Bb3 exd4. **7. Bd5** (7. Nxd4? Nxd4 8. Qxd4 c5 9. Qd5 Be6 10. Qc6+ Bd7 11. Qd5 c4 is the Noah's Ark trap; White could also play in gambit style, with 7. c3 dxc3 8. Nxc3 [*8. Qd5 Qd7 is not convincing.*])

170

Deflection Sacrifice

Intermediate Position 12

Kopec - A. Ivanov
Eastern Class Championships, 1994
White to move

12. **1.Rf8+!** (1. Qg8+ is also good but not as quick: 1. ... Kf6 2. Rxc7 Rxc7 3. Qd8+) **1. ... Kxf8 2. Qxg6**.

171

**Intermediate
Position 13**

Black to move

Accelerated Sicilian,
Book Trap

This arises after the opening moves 1. e4 c5 2. Nf3 Nc6 3. d4 cxd4 4. Nxd4 g6 5. Nc3 Bg7 6. Be3 Nf6 7. Bc4 Qa5 8. f3. **8. ... Qb4 9. Bb3 Nxe4**

wins a pawn. This is a book trap from the Accelerated Fianchetto Variation of the Sicilian Defense.

172

**Intermediate
Position 14**

White to move

King Ahead of Pawn

1. Kd4 is the only move to win. To win the ending K + P vs. K you must have the opposition ahead of the pawn. Here White ensures his King will get two ranks ahead of the pawn (which always wins with a non-rook pawn) and is well on the way to "building a bridge" for the pawn to "walk" through.

173

Sicilian Defense,
Opening Trap

This arises after the
opening moves 1. e4
c5 2. Nf3 d6 3. d4 cxd4
4. Nxd4 Nf6 5. Nc3
Nc6 6. Bc4 Bd7 7. Be3?
Ng4 8. Bc1?. **8. ... Qb6**
This is a trap which I
(DK) have employed a

Intermediate
Position 15
Pseudo-Dragon
Variation
Canadian Open,
Toronto 1976
Rd10, Nadeau-Kopec
Black to move

number of times for Black. **9. Be3** (9. Nd5 Qxd4 10. Qxd4 Nxd4) **9.
... Nxe3 10. fxe3 Ne5 11. Nd5 Qd8**

174

Decoy, Classic
Bishop Sacrifice

1. Bxc3! Successful
chess play is largely
based on being able to
recognize and exploit
well known patterns.
Here White has recog-

Intermediate
Position 16
White to move

nized an original opportunity to employ a variation of the Classic
Bishop Sacrifice. **1. ... Qxc3 2. Bxh7+ Kxh7** (In the game, play continued 2. ... Kh8 3. Qh3 etc. when White had a continuing and
vicious attack which chased the Black King all over the board. This
occurred in Kopec - Fedorowicz, Phillips and Drew Knights,
London, 1982.) **3. Ng5+**

175

Intermediate
Position 17

Hal Terrie
Original, 2002
Black to move

Knight vs. Bad Bishop

1. ... Bxd3 2. Kxd3 Kd5.
This is the cleanest way, seizing the central square for the king. (2. ... Ne7 3. Ke4 b5 4. Kf4 allows White too much play.) **3. Bg5** Preventing the immediate Ne7-f5. **3. ... Na7** Clearly best, threatening both ... Nc6 and ... Nb5. (3. ... b5 would be a mistake, as Black would have no pawn tempi after that. Black might still win but it would not be easy at all.) **4. Bc1** To answer ... Nb5 with Bb2 but now ... (4. a4 Nc6 just loses a pawn immediately.) **4. ... Nc6 5. Be3 Ne7 6. Bg1** (6. a4 Nc6 7. b5 axb5 8. axb5 Na7 9. b6 Nc8 wins the pawn at last.) **6. ... Nf5 7. Bf2 b5** Finally the moment comes to use that pawn move! White is in *zugzwang* — he has no move which will not fatally compromise his position. **8. Kc3 Ke4** and Black wins.

176

Intermediate
Position 18

White to move

Discovery,
Double Attack

This arises after the opening moves 1. e4 c5 2. Nf3 d6 3. Bc4 Nc6 4. 0-0 Bg4 (?) This move is weak as White can already play 5.Bxf7+ etc. but it leads to our intended example position. 5. c3 Ne5. **6. Nxe5!** Black has just played ... Ne5 trying to exploit the pin on f3. However Black has neglected development and the safety of his king. **6. ... Bxd1** (6. ... dxe5 7. Qxg4 with an extra piece.)

177

Complex
Opposition Theme

Intermediate
Position 19

White to move

Dedrle, 1921

1. Kb1! (1. Kc3? a3 2.
bxa3 only draws, as
Black reaches the c8
square: [2. *b3 Ke5 3. b4
a2 4. Kb2 a1Q+ 5. Kxa1 Kd4 6. Kb2 Kc4 7. Ka3 Kb5* is only a draw,
because White is not in front of his pawn with opposition.] 2. ...
Ke7 3. Kb4 Kd7 4. Kb5 Kc8= — another piece of specific endgame
knowledge that advanced players must have.) **1. ... Ke5** (1. ... a3 2.
b3 [Of course not 2. *bxa3??* which once again allows a draw. Also
2. b4? Ke6 3. Ka2 Kd6 4. Kxa3 Kc6 5. Ka4 Kb6 is a draw.] 2. ... Ke5 3.
Ka2 Kd5 4. Kxa3 Kc6 [4. ... *Kc5 5. Ka4*] 5. Ka4! The "diagonal opposition." [*Not 5. Kb4? Kb6* and Black draws.]) **2. Ka2 Kd4 3. Ka3 Kc5
4. Kxa4** and the White king is two ranks ahead of the WP. White
wins.

178

Decoy Sacrifice

1. ... Rxe4! Black's decoy sacrifice forces the
exposure of the White
king. **2. Rxe4 Qf2+ 3.
Ng2 Nf3+ 4. Kh1
Nxg3#.**

Intermediate
Position 20

Livshits-Kopec,
Toronto, 1993

Black to move

179

Intermediate Position 21

Black to move

Evans Gambit, Book Trap

This position arises after the opening moves 1. e4 e5 2. Nf3 Nc6 3. Bc4 Bc5 4. b4 Bxb4 5. c3 Ba5 6. d4 d6 7. Qb3. **7. ... Qd7** is the only move which defends against the threat of winning a piece with d5. This is a book position from the Evans Gambit. (7. ... Qe7 8. d5 Nb8 9. Qa4+; 7. ...Qf6 8. d5 Nb8 9. Qa4+. This position again demonstrates that sometimes you must have specific opening knowledge. Sometimes due to hidden tactical possibilities this cannot be avoided.)

180

Intermediate Position 22

Kopec-Bellin
Edinburgh Open
Scotland, 1981
White to move

Accurate Simplification

1. Rxc6 is the most precise, simplifying to an immediate *win:* (After 1. Rxb7 Rxb7 [*1. ... Bxd6? 2. Rxf7 Kxf7 3. Kd5; 1. ... Rxd6 still holds on*] 2. Rxb7 Bxd6 3. Kd5 Rc7 4. Rb6 Be7 White is winning but Black can still make some moves. In other words, White should win, but he may have to play for a number of more moves and hours.) **1. ... bxc6 2. Rb8+ Kd7 3. Rb7+ Ke8 4. Rxf7 Kxf7 5. Bxc5** with the devastating threat of d7. This was the conclusion of Kopec - Bellin, Second Edinburgh Congress, 1981.The endgame usually occurs after a number of hours of play. Hence, when a simplifying combination is available whereby you can convert to an "easier" endgame, it is important to find it.

181

Knight Decoy
with Intermezz 10

1. ... Ng5! A surprising
and effective tactical
blow. Retreating N
moves or retreating
moves on a long diag-
onal are often over-
looked. **2. Nxg5** (2.
Qe2 Nxf3+ (also ...
Nxh3+). 3. Qxf3 Qe1+
4. Qf1 Qxe3+) **2. ...
Qxe3+ 3. Kh1 fxg5.**

**Intermediate
Position 23**
Rajna-Kopec,
World Chess Festival
New Brunswick, 1988
Black to move

182

Prevent Counterplay

1. Rd8+ (Prevent
counterplay! After 1.
Rxf7+? Ke8 Black has
dangerous threats. For
example 2. Ra7 hxg2+
3. Kg3 g1Q+! 4. Rxg1
Bc8) **1. ... Kg7 2. Rxh8**

**Intermediate
Position 24**
Kopec-Gerzadowicz
1991-Friendly
Correspondence
Game
White to move

Kxh8 3. Bxf7 (3. Kxh3) **3. ... hxg2 4. Bxg6 Re2** (4. ... Rf2 5. Be4 b4
6. axb4 Rxb2 7. e6 Bb5 8. Rd5 Rxb4 9. e7) **5. Be4** Again, the les-
son is that in chess, particularly in the ending, it is important to
find variations which can translate a good or won position into
one where your opponent actually resigns.

Conclusion

Chess is an excellent game for cognitive development and for the exercise of cognitive skills. In this volume, using seven tests and 182 examples, our purpose has been three-fold:

(1)   to test your chess skills;

(2)   to evaluate your chess knowledge; and

(3)   to enable you to learn, increase your knowledge, and improve your chess play.

Readers can derive a clearer picture of their performance on the tests by totaling their difficulty scores. A score of 90% or better (of the maximum total) would indicate mastery of the material.

Future efforts will concentrate on the study of performance on individual questions with breakdown by topic areas and by level of ability.

We hope that you find we have fulfilled our mission.

Appendix 1

Experiments in Chess Cognition

D. Kopec, M. Newborn, and W. Yu
School of Computer Science, McGill University, Montreal, Canada

Abstract

The results of three related studies measuring the performance of humans and computer chess programs on different test positions are analyzed. The three experiments are: (1) The Pairs Experiment, (2) The Computer Test and (3) The Time Sequence Experiment. The underlying theme of all the work reported is oriented towards addressing the question: "How does the performance of humans and computer chess programs on a set of problem positions vary with time?" There are some surprisingly tangible results.

Introduction

In general there are two methods of remedy when a computer is insufficiently fast to handle a given problem in an acceptable time. The more common, simpler solution is to switch to a more powerful machine. However, this approach is not always feasible, and the fastest computer is not fast enough for some tasks.

The second solution is to employ more than one processor of the same family to work concurrently. In the ideal situation, the number of processors employed is inversely proportional to the required computation time. However, the processors must communicate with each other and the subprocesses must be synchronized. Thus as the number of processors increases, the margin of their increase in computation power decreases. The program

OSTRICH (Newborn, 1982) uses eight Data General Nova computers in parallel. Each Nova computer is able to search one lookahead subtree. A master processor receives results from all the other processors and then selects the best one.

The pairs experiment is an attempt to discover whether humans, operating in pairs, perform significantly better than they would alone. A positive result from this experiment would be interesting, since humans do not have the capability to interact as efficiently as closely coupled computers, and are not likely to be able to subdivide their analysis to avoid overlapping work. The experiment is discussed in detail below.

The computer test is an updated version of the Bratko-Kopec Test (Bratko and Kopec 1982), and provides a background to the pairs experiment by providing a technique for measuring chess ability and examining the differences between tactical positions (which can be solved by very little chess knowledge plus searching), and lever positions (which require more knowledge). Lever positions are also taken to be representative of positional problems in general, in that some appropriate chess knowledge is required and no reasonable amount of search effort using an evaluation, without that knowledge, could solve the problem.

THE PAIRS EXPERIMENT

Experimental Design

Fifty-eight positions are used in this experiment (see Appendix A for the complete set). The experiment is divided into three phases. In phase 1, each subject is given eight practice positions. In phases 2 and 3, each subject and each pair of subjects are tested on 25 positions. The positions are divided into three sets: the set consisting of eight positions for the practice phase, and two sets of 25 positions each for the main phase.

Each subject's performance on the last five positions of the practice set was scored for pairing purposes only. Subjects were paired in score order from highest to lowest. The pairs were then divided into two groups, A and B, of approximately equal size. All subjects in Group A had higher scores in phase 1 of the experiment than any subjects in Group B.

In phase 2, Group A took one of the main sets of positions in pairs. Both members of each pair were encouraged to discuss each test position together, thereby discouraging domination by either partner throughout the test set. At the same time, Group B took the other set of positions as individuals. For phase 3, the groups swap the position sets, with Group A working as individuals while Group B worked in pairs. In both phases 2 and 3, the first 5 positions were treated as further practice, and only the remaining twenty scored. Two minutes were allowed for each position.

The experiment is based on the earlier Bratko-Kopec experiment, though here only human chessplayers were tested. All positions are tactical (T) or lever (L) problems. Small differences compared to the earlier test are the subjects (or pairs) were asked to do 25 positions, instead of 24, and that the first five were not scored, being present only for practice. Thus the test consisted of 20 positions, 10 type T and 10 type L, compared to the 24 positions, 12 T and 12 L, of the earlier Bratko-Kopec test. Scores, for individuals or pairs, were out of a maximum of 20.

Learning factors for subjects may play a role in this experiment. One possibility was that the subjects might improve their ability during the experiment as a result of gaining familiarity with the types of position being used. On the other hand, another possibility was that subjects might become fatigued and their performance might decrease as the experiment proceeded. These possibilities prompted the arrangement whereby half of the subjects work in pairs first, and half work as individuals first. With this arrangement, any learning or fatigue effects will tend to cancel themselves out in the overall results.

Results of the Experiment

The main objective of this experiment, to ascertain how the performance of pairs compare to that of individuals, was achieved, and the overall conclusion is that a pair of subjects will perform significantly better than their average performance as individuals.

The improvement in pair's scores was mainly due to an improvement in the L-factor of their scores, though throughout the experiment the T-factor also improves slightly. Tables 1 and 2 indicate that L scores for pairs improved over L scores for individuals in each of 5 rating categories. Tables 3 and 4 indicate that overall scores for all pairs, whether low-rated, intermediate, or high-rated, tended to benefit from cooperation.

We tested 44 subjects, two of whom only did phases 1 and 2 of the experiment, leaving us with complete test results on 42 subjects. The distribution of the 44 individual scores on T and L within six rating categories is given in Table 1. The distribution of 21 subject pairs is given in Table 2. The rating allocated for a subject pair is the average of the individual ratings.

Table 1
Average Individual Scores

Rating Range	Mean T	Mean L	Mean TS	Mean 10(T-L)/S	Number of Subjects	Standard Deviation of TS
1000-1599	1.88	1.29	3.17	0.73	8	2.07
1600-1799	3.25	2.68	5.93	0.48	12	2.39
1800-1999	4.01	4.64	8.65	-0.57	11	2.54
2000-2199	4.40	4.24	8.63	0.14	11	2.45
2200-2399	7.00	8.50	15.50	-15.00	1	0.00
2400 +	8.00	9.00	17.00	-10.00	1	0.00
Overall:	4.63	4.61	9.24	-1.09	44	

Table 2
Average Pairs Scores

Rating Range	Mean T	Mean L	Mean TS	Mean 10(T-L)/S	Number of Pairs	Standard Deviation of TS
1000-1599	2.67	3.61	6.28	-3.14	3	0.77
1600-1799	3.06	4.04	7.09	-1.09	9	2.35
1800-1999	6.30	4.83	11.14	4.90	3	1.16
2000-2199	6.97	6.90	13.85	0.14	5	0.99
2200-2399	7.00	10.00	17.00	-30.00	1	0.00
Overall:	5.20	5.88	11.07	-5.84		

"Mean T" and "Mean L" scores in Tables 1 and 2 are out of 10, and "Mean TS" scores are out of 20. The proportional deviation "(T-L)/S" (computed to determine whether there are differences between performance on type T and type L positions) is multiplied by 10 for scaling purposes.

Table 3
Pair Improvement: Percentages for T, L and Overall

Rating Range	Improvement in T (%)	Improvement in L (%)	Improvement in TS (%)
1000-1599	42.2	179.6	98.2
1600-1799	-06.0	50.8	19.7
1800-1999	57.0	4.1	28.7
2000-2199	58.5	62.7	60.5
2200-2399	00.0	17.6	9.7

Table 4
Pair Improvement: Overall Totals

Rating Range	Mean Individual TS	Mean Pair TS	Mean Improvement
1000-1599	3.17	6.28	3.11
1600-1799	5.93	7.09	1.17
1800-1999	8.65	11.14	2.48
2000-2199	8.63	13.85	5.22
2200-2399	15.50	17.00	1.50

Pair Improvements

We composed by extrapolation a rating score table for this experiment from the earlier Bratko-Kopec experiment. Given a rating category, one could expect scores to fall within the ranges indicated in Table 5.

Table 5

Rating	Score
1300-1599	0-4
1600-1799	5-6
1800-1999	7-8
2000-2199	09-12
2200-2399	13-16
2400 +	17-20

From Table 5 and the results listed in Tables 1 and 2, we constructed Table 6, which shows the average increase in scores and rating points for pairs over individuals.

Table 6

Rating Category	Increase in Score From Individual to Pair	Estimated Rating Point Improvement
1300-1599	3.0	250
1600-1799	1.2	100
1800-1999	2.5	200
2000-2199	5.2	250
2200-2399	1.5	100 (only 1 pair)

Table 6 shows that the rating for a pair is typically in the category above the rating category for the individuals. The average improvement approaches 200 rating points.

Statistical Analysis

We can use an F test to examine the negative hypothesis that pair scores are no better (i.e. have the same mean and variance) than the average of the individual scores of the subjects comprising the pair.

Let $s_1 \ldots s_n$ be the pairs' scores
$a_1 \ldots a_n$ be the average of the 2 individual scores.
Writing $d_i = s_i - a_i$ with mean D;
V (the variance) $= 1 / (n - 1) \Sigma (d_i - D)^2$
and the statistic $F^2 = nD^2/V$ has an F(1, n-1) distribution.

On the data for the 21 pairs (given in Appendix 1-a), calculation gives:

$n = 21$ $D = 2.25$ $V = 12.33$ $F^2 = 8.65$

Since F(1,20) at the 99% confidence level is 8.10, we can conclude with greater than 99% confidence, that the hypothesis that pair scores are no better can be rejected; and thus that the substantial improvement in pair scores is statistically significant.

Discussions with cognitive psychologists led to the suggestion that our experiment may have included built-in bias. Pair scores may have been superior to the average of the pair's individual scores because the strongest member of the pair was choosing the move and the other member was complying with the first member's choice. Although this is conceivable, it wouldn't explain pair scores higher than the strongest member's scores on the individual test. In fact, in 13 out of the 16 cases where pair scores were higher than the average of the individual scores, the pair score was also higher than the greater of the individual scores.

The strongest version of the "better player dominates" suggestion leads to the idea of a "composite maximum" score (CM). The CM is a hypothetical score computed from the individual results. It is calculated by summing, over all positions, the better score on each position separately. It provides a measure of the pair score that might result if, without any genuine cooperation in problem solving, the pair somehow always managed to choose between their two answers in favor of the correct one, if any.

The statistical analysis of our experiment showed that, with very high confidence, pair scores are better than individual scores. Unfortunately, possibly because of the limited sample size, our data does not permit us to demonstrate that pair scores are better than the "composite maximum" scores.

As so much data on human scores was available, a regression and analysis of variance test was carried out to examine the basic assumption of the Bratko-Kopec test, namely that the scores on these tests correlate with chess rating. For the individual scores, a value of 52 with $F(1,42)$ distribution was obtained for the negative hypothesis of no correlation, and for the pairs a value of 43 with $F(1,19)$ distribution. This confirms the correlation at a highly satisfactory level (greater than 99% confidence).

THE COMPUTER TEST

Following the 1983 World Computer Chess Championship, we sent two test sets of 25 positions each to the 22 participants. One test set was almost identical (two positions discarded and three added) to the earlier Bratko-Kopec experiment and was labeled "Old Positions", and the other set was labeled "New Positions." The results of ten computer programs on the Old Positions and 15 programs on the New Positions are given in Table 7a and 7b. The column "SS" gives the total score on all 25 positions of the test, and the column "S" represents the total score on the last 20 positions on each test, and is thus useful for comparison with human results (e.g. in the pairs experiment) where only 20 positions were scored. In each test, the last 20 positions consisted of ten tactical and ten lever positions, and the columns "T" and "L" represent the tactical and lever components of "S." Of the "Old Position" results, eight of the ten programs were new to the Bratko-Kopec Test. All the programs, regardless of their ratings, score relatively highly when compared with humans (Table 4). Most probably some of these scores do not represent true Bratko-Kopec test scores, but rather the result of its use as a training set.

Table 7a
Computer Test Results: Old Positions

Name		Est. Rating	SS	TT	LL	S	T	L	10* (T-L)/S
Pion	S	1349	6.8	5.8	1.0	5.8	4.8	1.0	+ 6.6
Const.	C	1816	12.0	8.0	4.0	9.0	6.0	3.0	+ 3.3
Bebe	S	1885	13.0	10.0	3.0	9.0	7.0	2.0	+ 5.6
Patsoc	M	1291	13.0	11.0	2.0	10.0	8.0	2.0	+ 6.0
Awit	M	1660	13.2	6.8	6.3	10.7	5.3	5.3	+ 0.0
Bobby	M	1186	14.0	7.0	7.0	11.0	6.0	5.0	+ 0.9
Phoenix	M	1780	14.3	7.0	7.3	11.8	6.0	5.8	+ 0.1
Adv.3.0	S	1900	17.0	9.0	8.0	13.5	8.0	5.5	+ 1.9
Belle	S	2200	18.3	11.0	7.3	14.3	9.0	5.3	+ 2.6
Merlin	M	1791	18.5	11.5	7.0	16.0	10.0	6.0	+ 2.5

Table 7b
Computer Test Results: Old Positions

Name		Est. Rating	SS	TT	LL	S	T	L	10* (T-L)/S
Spinks	M	1000	4.0	2.0	2.0	4.0	2.0	2.0	+ 0.0
Pion	S	1349	6.1	3.3	2.6	5.0	2.8	2.3	+ 1.0
Const.	C	1816	7.1	5.8	1.3	6.8	5.5	1.3	+ 6.1
Bobby	M	1186	7.5	4.0	3.5	5.5	3.0	2.5	+ 0.9
BCP	m	1260	8.0	6.0	2.0	8.0	4.5	3.5	+ 1.3
Patsoc	M	1291	8.0	4.0	4.0	7.0	4.0	3.0	+ 1.4
Awit	M	1660	9.2	5.8	3.3	7.8	5.5	2.3	+ 4.1
Adv.3.0	S	1900	9.8	5.3	4.5	8.0	4.5	3.5	+ 1.3
Phoenix	M	1780	11.2	6.0	5.2	9.2	4.0	5.2	- 1.3
Bebe	S	1885	12.0	7.0	5.0	10.0	5.0	5.0	+ 0.0
Merlin	M	1791	12.3	5.3	7.0	10.0	5.0	5.0	+ 0.0
Belle	S	2200	17.9	10.3	7.6	13.7	7.3	6.3	+ 0.7

Key: T, L and S are scores from the last 20 positions, and may be compared with human results. TT, LL and SS are over all 25 positions. T and TT are totals for tactical positions; L and LL, totals for lever positions; S and SS overall totals.

> S: special purpose hardware
> M: Mainframe
> m: microprocessor
> C: commercial product

The column labeled "10*(T-L)/S" (the proportional deviation) indicates a consistent tendency for computer programs to score better on T positions than L positions. Scores for the "New Positions" are rather similar in distribution to those on the original Bratko-Kopec test and generally correspond to rating, particularly within rating categories. On this test set the domination of T over L is not as evident as in the earlier test, although the general trend is still apparent in the "10*(T-L)/S" column.

Partial credit for the 2nd, 3rd and 4th choices was obtained either directly from the program's output at the end of two minutes of "think" time, or from output of the "preferred move" after different periods of time, e.g. three minutes, 30 seconds, and one minute for 2nd, 3rd and 4th choices respectively. For all programs, most points scored were derived from the main preferred move (after two minutes computation). Where programs gave secondary moves, it was not always by the same method. It would have been more favorable for the experiment if all programs derived further choices in the same way.

TIME SEQUENCE EXPERIMENT

Objective of the Time Sequence Experiment

The purpose of this experiment is to obtain data which might give some insight as to how the performance of humans on sets of problem positions varies with time. The humans' performance is also compared on the basis of rating. The performance of computer chess programs on the same test sets over different time allocations is evaluated. The effect of employing two or more processors at the same time to attempt to solve these problem positions is also considered.

Design of the Experiment

A series of six test sets was devised and comprised three practice positions at two minutes each, four test sets of 10 positions devised/selected for 30 seconds, one minute, two minutes and four minutes of solution time each. Thus, the complete experimental sequence consists of 48 positions which when administered with a 15-minute break period, requires just over two hours. The test sets were administered in a predetermined, not strictly increasing or decreasing time order, which varied with each group of subjects tested, e.g. the last group of six subjects was tested in the order practice, four minutes, two minutes, break, 30 seconds, one minute, eight minutes. A total of 22 subjects with Quebec Chess Federation ratings between 1453 and 2358 (one rated below 1600, ten rated between 1600 and 2000, ten rated between 2000 and 2299, and one rated over 2300) were tested. They were randomly chosen from chessplayers in these rating categories in the Montreal area.

Results of the Experiment

Detailed results are given in Appendix C. Table 8 summarizes the results by rating category. Subjects fell into two major rating categories: 1600-1999 (ten subjects) and 2000-2299 (ten subjects). One significant trend emerges. On the four-minute and eight-minute test sets the 2000-2299 subjects scored 20.1% and 17.4% respectively, above the 1600-1999 subjects, while on the 30-second, one-minute and two-minute test sets the scores of the two groups differed by less than 8%. Figure 1 shows this trend diagramatically.

Table 8
Average results by rating category

Rating Range	30 sec.%	1 min.%	2 min.%	4 min.%	8 min.%	Total
less than 1600	25.0	5.0	40.0	40.0	5.0	21.11
1600-1999	38.7	52.3	40.2	26.6	49.6	40.57
2000-2299	46.6	57.9	41.7	46.7	67.0	50.31
2300 & greater	45.0	66.7	70.0	25.0	100.0	57.04
Overall	38.8	45.5	48.0	25.8	64.2	42.27
% Change Intermediate to Strong	7.9	5.6	1.5	20.1	17.4	9.74

Figure 1
Performance Variation with Time

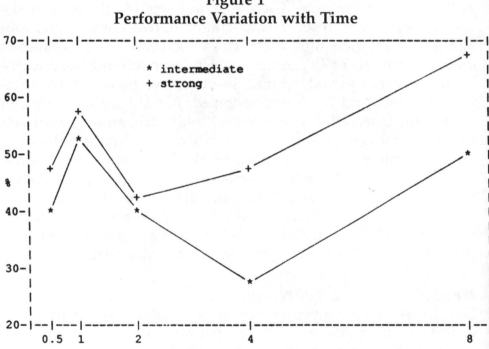

Statistical analyses (T test and analysis of variance) uniformly detected a significant difference between the average scores of the intermediate and strong groups for the four-minute and eight-minute test sets, but not for the two-minute, one-minute or 30-second tests. This result suggests that the stronger chessplayers distinguish themselves over the intermediate ones when given longer periods of time to solve their problem positions. That is, with more time they can develop the deep understanding of a position which is necessary to solve it, whereas on the shorter term test sets (30-seconds, one-minute, two-minutes) their performance is rather similar to the intermediate players. This finding is in line with the findings of Chase and Simon (1973).

Results from Computer Programs

The positions used for the time sequence experiment on humans, except for the practice positions, were input to three computer programs: two versions of the program OSTRICH using one processor and seven processors in parallel, respectively; and the commercial microcomputer program CONSTELLATION which employs only one processor.

The results are given in Appendix 1-C. The following conclusions can be drawn:

(1) There is no significant difference between the two versions of OSTRICH. It should be mentioned that for certain positions in which the seven processor version of OSTRICH failed, the version using one processor chose the preferred move.

(2) The results obtained by CONSTELLATION are slightly better than those obtained by both versions of OSTRICH, but the difference is not statistically significant.

(3) All the programs behave like weak chessplayers. That is, they have reasonably high test scores in the test set with the shortest time (30 seconds) and they perform very poorly in the other test sets. They cannot find the preferred move in the cases where knowledge is required (e.g. deep strategical concepts, non-standard sacrifices). It should be noted that in the test sets with the longest solution times (4 min-

utes and 8 minutes), in those few cases where a program found the preferred move, it was found in a very short time (e.g. in one or two minutes).

Acknowledgments

We would like to thank Professor Guy Groen, of the Department of Educational Psychology, McGill University, for interesting discussions and advice regarding our experimental design and the analysis of results; as well as Professor Tony Marsland of the University of Alberta, Edmonton, for useful comments. We would like to thank all those who assisted this research, in particular Sylvia Kopec, Daniel Lavellee, Alec Sandy and Elizabeth Vinceller, as well as Linda Pilkington for typing and administrative assistance; and not in the least, the School of Computer Science, McGill University, for making this research possible.

References

Chase, W.G. and Simon, H.A., *Perception in Chess*. Cog. Psych. 4, pp. 55-81, 1973.

Elo, A., *The Rating of Chessmasters—Past and Present*. Batsford, London, 1978.

Draper, N.R. and Smith, N., *Applied Regression Analysis*. John Wiley & Sons, New York, 1967.

deGroot, A. (edited by G.W. Baylor), *Thought and Choice in Chess*. Mouton, The Hague (and Paris), 1965. (Translation and additions from the original 1946 Dutch edition.)

Hort, V. and Jansa, V., *The Best Move*, RHM Press, New York, 1980. (Translation and additions from the original 1976 Russian edition.)

Huntsberger, D.V. and Billingsley, P., *Elements of Statistical Inference*. Allyn and Bacon Inc., Boston, 1977.

Kopec, D. and Bratko, I., *The Bratko-Kopec Experiment: A Comparison of Human and Computer Performance in Chess*. In: Advances in Computer Chess 3, pp. 57-72, M.R.B. Clarke, editor. Pergamon Press, Oxford, 1982.

Kopec, D., Irazoqui, E. and Bratko, I., *The Updated Bratko-Kopec Test*. In Computer Chess Digest Annual, pp. 45-63, E. Irazoqui, editor. Computer Chess Digest Inc., Huntington, New York, 1983.

Lasker, E., *Lasker's Manual of Chess*. Dover, New York, 1947.

Matanovic, A., *Informator No. 18* (Center Za unapredivanja saha), Belgrade 1975.

Newborn, M., *OSTRICH/P—a parallel search chess program*. Tech. Rep. 82.3, School of Computer Science, McGill University, Montreal, P.Q., 1982.

Nievergelt, J., *Information Content of Chess Positions: Implications for Chess Specific Knowledge of Chessplayers*. SIGART Newsletter 62, pp. 13-15, 1977.

Pachman, L., *Modern Chess Tactics*. Routledge & Kegan Paul, London, 1973.

(Translation by P.H. Clarke from the original 1970 Czech edition.)

Pritchett, C. and Kopec, D., *Best Games of the Young Grandmasters.* Bell & Hyman, London, 1980.

Shannon, H.A., *Programming a Computer for Playing Chess,* Philos. Mag. 7th Ser. 41, pp. 256-275, 1959.

Wade, R. and O'Connell, K. (Eds), *Bobby Fischer's Chess Games.* Doubleday & Co., London, 1972.

Appendix 1-a

Positions Used in the Pairs Experiment

Fifty-eight positions were used; eight for the practice session and 25 each for the main tests. The revised Bratko-Kopec Test provided 50 of them (25 "old" and 25 "new," making them almost identical to the positions in the first two tests given in this book), and an additional eight positions were selected for practice, not given here.

Subject Pairing Chart

Practice Scores were used for pairing. Pairs were formed by matching performances on the last five of the practice positions in score order from high to low.

Name (Rating[1], Practice Score)			
1. Spraggett	(2542, 4.33)	Levtchouk	(2209, 4.00)
2. Quance	(1870, 3.33)	Finta	(2102, 2.00)
3. Kowalski	(1500, 2.33)	Kurtz	(2113, 2.00)
4. Beaudry	(1797, 2.00)	Duchoeny	(1793, 2.00)
5. Chauvet	(1679, 2.00)	M. Arsenault	(1780, 2.00)
6. Proulx	(1800, 2.00)	Morin	(1900, 1.75)
7. Ruggeri	(1500, 2.00)	Fata	(1849, 1.50)
8. Demers	(1750, 1.50)	Michaud	(1770, 1.50)
9. Roy	(2034, 1.50)	Rousseau	(2126, 1.00)
10. Zurowski	(2129, 1.50)	Roos	(2150, 1.33)
11. Martinez	(1728, 1.33)	Desforges	(1975, 1.00)
12. J. Jacques	(1860, 1.00)	Grigorion	(1670, 1.00)
13. Szwaronek	(1750, 1.00)	D. Arsenault	(1815, 1.00)
14. Smith	(1450, 1.00)	Boulay	(1421, 1.00)
15. Maison	(1600, 0.50)	Sirois	(1350, 0.50)
16. Beaudoin	(1460, 0.00)	Geoffrey	(1700, 0.00)
17. Sack	(1800, 0.00)[2]	Wang	(1986)
18. Moser	(1600, 0.00)[2]	Strothotte	(1815, 0.00)
19. R. Jacques	(1500, 0.50)	Leclare[3]	
20. Dupuis	(2042)	M. Williams	(1475)
21. Pineault	(2059)	Sasseville	(2088)
22. Nadeau	(2120)	L. Williams	(2173)

1 Quebec Chess Federation rating 1983 (except as indicated by note 2).

2 Official rating not available, estimated rating only.

3 Dummy pair due to odd number of subjects. Results of this pair will not be counted.

Pair Results (In Ascending Score Order)

#.	Name	Rating	\<Pair Scores\> T	L	S	\<Individual Scores\> T	L	S	CM
1.	Duchoeny	1801	1.50	2.50	**4.00**	6.00	4.50	**10.50**	11.50
	Beaudry	1797				4.50	3.50	**8.00**	
2.	Fata	1980	3.50	1.50	**5.00**	2.33	6.00	**18.33**	9.33
	Ruggeri	1500				3.00	3.33	**5.33**	
3.	Boulay	1355	3.00	2.50	**5.50**	2.00	1.50	**3.50**	4.50
	Smith	1450				0.00	1.00	**1.00**	
4.	Maison	1600	2.00	4.00	**6.00**	2.00	0.00	**2.00**	3.50
	Sirois	1320				1.50	0.00	**1.50**	
5.	Moser	1700	1.00	5.00	**6.00**	4.00	4.00	**8.00**	12.50
	Strothotte	1800				1.50	3.50	**5.00**	
6.	Michaud	1812	2.50	4.00	**6.50**	4.00	3.00	**7.00**	10.50
	Demers	1681				2.00	2.00	**4.00**	
7.	Kurtz	2050	2.00	4.50	**6.50**	6.50	6.15	**12.66**	13.80
	Kowalski	1500				3.00	3.50	**6.50**	
8.	M. Arsenault	1820	3.00	3.50	**6.50**	5.00	6.00	**11.00**	13.50
	Chauvet	1638				6.00	1.00	**7.00**	
9.	Geoffrey	1715	3.00	4.33	**7.33**	0.00	2.50	**2.50**	2.50
	Beaudoin	1460				0.00	0.00	**0.00**	
10.	Szwaronek	1739	3.50	4.33	**7.85**	4.00	2.50	**6.50**	8.00
	D. Arsenault	1815				3.00	3.33	**6.33**	
11.	Dupuis	2042	4.00	5.00	**9.00**	3.50	2.50	**6.00**	8.50
	M. Williams	1500				2.50	1.00	**3.50**	
12.	Proulx	1780	5.66	4.00	**9.66**	5.00	6.00	**11.00**	12.80
	Morin	1885				3.00	3.15	**6.15**	
13.	Wang	1900	6.25	5.00	**11.25**	2.00	8.50	**10.50**	12.00
	Sack	1800				4.00	4.00	**8.00**	
14.	Martinez	1806	7.00	5.50	**12.50**	3.00	4.00	**7.00**	9.50
	Desforges	1899				3.00	1.00	**4.00**	
15.	Joannisse	1850	6.50	6.00	**12.50**	5.33	3.74	**9.10**	12.25
	Gregorion	1670				3.00	2.80	**5.80**	
16.	Pineault	2059	6.00	6.50	**12.50**	3.00	3.00	**6.00**	10.50
	Sasseville	2088				2.90	3.00	**5.90**	
17.	Rousseau	2105	6.00	7.00	**13.00**	2.33	7.00	**9.33**	12.80
	Roy	2023				5.50	2.33	**7.80**	
18.	Zurowski	2129	7.00	7.00	**14.00**	5.50	3.50	**9.00**	10.50
	Ross	2021				4.00	2.50	**6.50**	
19.	Quance	1945	7.85	6.75	**14.50**	6.50	7.20	**13.60**	17.33
	Pinta	2085				5.33	8.00	**13.33**	
20.	Nadeau	2120	8.00	7.25	**15.25**	3.90	5.33	**9.20**	12.66
	L. Williams	2173				5.90	3.33	**9.20**	
21.	Spraggett	2538	7.00	10.00	**17.00**	8.00	9.00	**17.00**	17.00
	Levtchouk	2209				7.00	8.50	**15.50**	

As mentioned in the main text, all test positions were chosen while trying to maintain a one to one ratio between T and L. The work reported by Kopec, Irazoqui and Bratko (1982) indicates that as chessplayers improve and become strong (over 2000), we can expect a corresponding improvement in their L scores. This general result was also seen in the pairs experiment, both for pairs and individuals. In fact, the improvement of scores of pairs over individuals is mostly as a result of improvement in L scores, although T scores also increased. Although in nearly all positions it was evident that there was only one best move, further analysis of positions and post-mortem discussion with some subjects suggested that perhaps some of the L positions were too sharp, tending too much towards T positions, whereas T positions did not necessarily result in the immediate win of material or checkmate (unlike those of the earlier Bratko-Kopec Test). Thus perhaps for the purpose of selecting test positions, two heads would have been better than one.

Appendix 1-b

Time Sequence Positions

The 45 scored (i.e. not practice) positions in the time sequence experiment are given below in a modified Forsythe notation. White pieces are in capital letters (K,Q,R,B,N,P) and Black pieces are given in lower case letters (k,q,r,b,n,p). All rows are given separately unless there is a series of empty rows, e.g. 32 means four empty rows. Positions are read left to right, top to bottom, i.e. from the a8 square to the h1 square.

30 seconds

1. (W) rn1qk2r; pbppbppp; 1p2pn; 8; 2PP1B; 4PN; PP3PPP; RN1QKB1R
2. (B) r5kb; 2p1n2p; q2p2rP; 1p1P1p; 1Q1NpPP; PP2N; K7; 3R3R
3. (W) 7K; 8; k1P;7p; 32
4. (B) r2qkb1r; pp1bpppp; 2np; 8; 2BNP1n; 2N; PPP2PPP; R1BQK2R
5. (W) r3rk; pq3p1p; 4p1Qpn; 1p; 2pP; 2P4R; PP3PbP; R5K
6. (W) r1b3r; pp2kq; 4pp1R; 3p; 2pP3Q; 2P3P; P1P1BP; 2KR
7. (W) rnbq1rk; pp1n2bp; 3pp1p; 2p; 4PP; 2NB1N; PPP3PP; R1BQ1RK
8. (B) 5k; 3b2p; 1pq4p; p1pPp1p; P1P1Pn; 2P; 2Q3PP; 3BB1K
9. (W) r4rk; 2pq2pp; p3bb; n2p2B; 2B; 2P2N; P3QPPP; R2R2K
10. (W) 8; p5pk; 6q; p6p; P6P; 8; 1KQ; 8

One Minute

1. (B) r1b2rk; pp1pn1bp; 2n1p1p; 4p; BqNP; 1P3N; P4PPP; R1BQR1K
2. (W) 2rq1r; ppnb1pbk; 2np2pp; 2p1p; P3P2P; 1BPPNN; 1P3PP; R1BQ1RK
3. (W) 6R; 2pk; P2p3p; 1P4p; 8; r5P; 7P; 6K
4. (B) rn1q1r1k; 1b2B1pp; p2pB; 8; Pp2n; 8; NPP2PPP; R2QR1K
5. (W) 3n; 1p1k3p; p1pbnpp; 4p; PP2PP1P; 1BPN1KP; 3B; 8
6. (B) r2r1nk; pqp1nppp; 1p2p; 1Q2P2P; 2PPR; 2B3N; P4PP; 5K1R
7. (W) r2kb1r; pp1n3p; 1qp1bpp; 3p1p; 3P; 2NBPQ1P; PPP1NPP; R3K2R
8. (B) r1bq2k; pp2p2p; 3p2p; 2p1n1B; P1B; 2n2P; 2PQ1P1P; R4RK
9. (B) 3k; 7K; 6r; 2KP; 32
10. (W) r1bqk2r; ppp1npbp; 3p1np; 3Pp; 2P1P1PP; 2N1B; PP3P; R2QKBNR

Two Minutes

1. (W) r3k1r; 1pqb1p; p1n1p; p3Pn; 1P1p1P; P2Q1N; 2P3PP; R1B1KB1R
2. (B) r1bqk; p1pn1pp; 1p3r; 2PPp; N3P1Pp; P2BQ2P; 3K1P; R6R
3. (W) 8; 1p1k; 1P; 2PK; 32
4. (B) r1b2rk; ppp2pp; 2n1pq1p; b2p; 2PP; PQNBPN; 1P3PPP; R3K2R
5. (W) r4rk; pp3ppp; 2p4q; 2P; 1b1P; 1B3NPb; PP2Q2P; R4RK
6. (W) 5r; 3q1kp; 1p2pr1p; 2p1R2P; p1PpQP; 6P; PPP; 2K1R
7. (B) r1bq1rk; pp1p1ppp; 4p; 2n; 2PQnB; P; 1P2PPPP; 3RKBNR
8. (W) 4rrk; 2q1bppp; p2p; 1p1Pn; 3B1R; P2B2Q; 1PP3PP; 5R1K
9. (W) 5k; 32; 2P; 8; 3K
10. (W) 3rr1k; 1p1bbp1p; p3p1p; q2nN1B; 3P; 2P4R; 4QPPP; 1B2R1K

Four Minutes

1. (B) rn2k2r; p1p2ppp; 1p2pn; 3q; 3P; 2PQP1N; P4PPP; R1B2K1R
2. (B) rn1q1rk; pb4pp; 1p1pp; 2pP1p; P1P; 2PBP; 2QB1PPP; R4RK
3. (W) r4rk; pp2qppp; 4b; 2p; 8; 4PQP; PP3PBP; R4RK
4. (B) rbqr1k; 5pbp; p1pp1np; 8; 1PPBP; 2N2P; P2QB1PP; 1R2K2R
5. (B) r3qr1k; 2p1ppbp; p1N3p; 2Q1P; 1p3B; 1P5b; 1PPR; 2K3R
6. (W) 5k; p1p4R; 1pr; 3p1pP; P2P1P; 2P2K; 16
7. (B) rnbqkbnr; ppp1p1pp; 8; 3p2N; 4p; 3P; PPP2PPP; RNBQKB1R
8. (W) 2r2r1k; ppq3bp; 5np; 3p; 4p1PP; 2PBBP; PP1Q; 1K1R3R
9. (B) 8; 6p; 7p; 5p; 4p2P; 4PkP; 5P; 4K
10. (W) 4rnk; 1bq3pp; p; 3nPQ; 1p; 1N1B; 6PP; 2B2R1K

Eight Minutes

1. (B) r3r1k; pp3pbp; 1qp3p; 2B; 2BP2b; Q1n2N; P4PPP; 3R1K1R
2. (W) 4r; pppk3p; 3pr; 5B; 16; PPP3PP; 4R1K
3. (B) r5rk; 1p1bqpnp; 3p1b1B; 1BnPp2P; 4P; 2N2Q; PP3P; R3KNR
4. (W) 2r2rk; pp2bp1p; 1qb1pnp; 3nN1B; 3P; P1NQ; BP3PPP; 2R2RK
5. (B) 24; 4n; 3K; 8; 6R; 3k

Solutions and Sources for the Time Sequence Experiment

Phase	To Move	Players and/or Source	Best Move
Practice, 2 minutes			
E	W	Timman-Garcia, B.G. p37	g3
O	W	Korchnoi-Tarjan, Lone Pine 1981	Bxg5
M	B	Sax-Ljubojevic, B.G. p192	b5
30 Seconds			
O	W	Miles-Spassky, B.G. p20	h3
M	B	Cooper-Hubner, Inf. 34 No. 25	Bxd4
E	W	Reti's Study, L.M. p161	c5

O ....B ....Nadeau-Kopec, Canadian Open 1976......................Qb6
M ....W ....Timman-Pomar, B.G. p48..Nf5
M ....W ....Forgacs-Spielmann, L.M. p172....................................f4
O ....W ....Fischer-Domnitz, B.F.C.G. p171 ....Ng5
M ....B ....Spassky-Fischer, Match, Reykjavik 1972 ....Bxa4
M ....W ....Fischer-Ree, B.F.C.G. p250, diag.169 ....Qxe6+
E..................W ....Study by Lasker, L.M. p155..Ka3

One Minute
M ....B ....Sax-Miles, B.G. p9 ....Rxf3
M ....W ....Kopec-Bellin, Edinburgh Congress 1981 ....h5
E..................W ....R+P ending, M.C. p190..b6
M ....B ....Gilden-Browne, B.G. p64 ....Qb6
E..................W ....Andersson-Chi, B.G. p108...f5
M ....B ....Gligoric-Portisch, O.P. p115.....................................Nf5
O ....W ....Browne-Byrne, B.G. p72...g4
M ....B ....Larsen-Browne, B.G. p66 ....e6
E..................B ....KRP vs. KR, M.C. p181 ....Rf6,Ra6,Ke8,Kc8
O ....W ....Polajzer-Davies, Graz, Austria 1981.....................Be2,f3

Two Minutes
O ....W ....Timman-Hug, B.G. p38..g4
M ....B ....Klugman-Kopec, World Open 1976 ....c6
E..................W ....Study, L.M. p155 ....Ke5
O ....B ..................M.C. p180 ....e5
M ....W ....Fischer-Minic, B.F.C.G. p264....................................Ne5
M ....W ....Kopec-Sun. Standard readers, M.C. p179 ....a3,Qh7
O ....B ....Quinteros-Ribli, B.G. p154......................................d5
M ....W ....Bednarski-Adamski, Inf. 26, No. 11......................Bxh7+
E..................W ....KPK endgame, A.C.C. 1, p112.................................Kc2
M ....W ....Browne-Zuckerman, B.G. p68..................................Nxf7

Four Minutes
O ....B ....Portisch-Gligoric, O.P. p114 ....Nbd7
M ....B ....Kopec-Fluk, M.C. p45..g6
M ....W ....Marshall-Capablanca, L.M. p175 ....e4
O ....B ....Lputyan-Kasparov, B.G. p199 ....c5
M ....B ....Vasjukov-Ribli, B.G. p158..a5
E..................W ....Capablanca-Tartakower, L.M. p217......................Kg3
O ....B ....Akesson-Leslie, European Junior, 1981 ....Qd6
M ....W ....Timman-Miles, B.G. p50...h5
E..................B ....Esser-Davidson, L.M. p147..f4
M ....W ....Prichett-Georghiu, London, 1980..............................Nc5

Eight Minutes

M ....B ....D. Byrne-Fischer, B.F.C.G. p111 ....Be6
E................W ....MacDonnell-Lewis, L.M. p174....................................c4
M ....B ....Speelman-Biyiasis, Inf. 26, No. 34 ....Nf4
M ....W ....deGroot-Scholtens, M.C. p64 ....Bxd5
E.................B ....KR vs. KN, Kopec study, A.C.C.2 p67 ....Nc6+

Abbreviations

B.F.C.G ...... *Bobby Fischer's Chess Games*, Wade and O'Connell
B.G. .... *Best Games of the Young Grandmasters*, Prichett and Kopec
M.C. .... *Mastering Chess*, Kopec et al.
L.M. .... *Lasker's Manual of Chess*, Emanual Lasker
O.P. .... *Opening Preparation*, Assiac and O'Connell
A.C.C.n ...... *Advances in Computer Chess*, Vol. n Ed: Clarke, M.R.B.
Inf.n .... *Informator* n Ed: Matanovic

Human Scores for the Time Sequence Experiment

#	Name	Rating*	P	30s	1min	2min	4min	8min	Total
2.	Chauvet	1636	0.0	4.00	5.00	3.83	2.17	2.00	17.00
3.	Duchoeny	1793	0.0	4.50	7.00	4.50	4.00	1.25	21.25
4.	Barre	1805	0.0	2.00	5.50	3.50	2.92	1.92	15.84
5.	Morin	1833	0.0	3.00	6.00	4.50	2.75	3.09	19.34
6.	Balla	1867	0.5	2.50	5.33	3.25	3.50	2.50	17.08
7.	Brodie	1900	0.5	4.50	5.75	3.33	2.25	1.50	17.33
8.	Fletcher	1901	0.0	4.00	5.50	3.00	2.00	3.00	17.50
9.	Desforges	1986	0.0	5.83	2.50	4.83	2.33	2.25	17.74
10.	Wang	1986	1.0	3.33	4.75	4.50	3.17	4.00	19.75
11.	Martinez	1990	1.0	5.00	5.00	5.00	1.50	3.25	19.75
12.	Roy	2050	0.5	4.50	5.00	5.83	3.83	3.25	22.41
13.	Dupuis	2062	0.0	1.00	4.50	5.00	3.00	2.00	15.50
14.	Bolduc	2080	0.0	4.00	5.00	3.50	7.42	4.00	23.92
15.	Alvarez	2041	1.0	2.00	2.75	5.50	3.75	4.00	18.00
16.	Rousseau	2105	1.0	4.25	5.67	3.67	5.50	4.00	23.09
17.	Lorenz	2108	0.5	5.00	5.50	2.00	3.67	1.50	17.67
18.	Ibrahim	2133	0.5	5.00	5.50	1.33	3.75	3.50	19.08
19.	Nadeau	2120	2.0	5.00	9.00	3.50	5.00	3.00	25.50
20.	Schaeffer	2236**	N/A	8.33	6.00	4.33	4.00	4.00	26.66
21.	Levtchouk	2261	2.0	7.50	9.00	7.00	6.75	4.33	34.58
22.	Coudari	2358	1.0	4.50	6.67	7.00	2.50	5.00	25.67

*Notes: * Quebec Chess Federation (FQE) rating.*

*** Canadian Rating (CFC).*

N/A = Data not available.

Computer Results for the Time Sequence Experiment

Program	30s	1 min	2 min	4 min	8 min	Total
1-Processor Ostrich	4.00	1.00	0.33	0.00	1.33	6.66
7-Processor Ostrich	5.00	0.50	0.25	0.50	1.00	7.25
Constellation	4.50	2.50	1.00	0.00	0.33	8.33

Second, third, and fourth choices for partial credit in the table above were obtained from non-standard solving times as follows:

Proper Time	2nd	3rd	4th
30 seconds	2 min	1 min	10 sec
1 minute	2 min	40 sec	20 sec
2 minutes	3 min	1 min	30 sec
4 minutes	5 min	2 min	1 min
8 minutes	4 min	2 min	1 min

Appendix 1-c

The Bratko-Kopec Test Revisited*

T. A. Marsland

1. Introduction

The twenty-four positions of the Bratko-Kopec test (Kopec and Bratko 1982) represent one of several attempts to quantify the playing strength of chess computers and human subjects. Although one may disagree with the choice of test set, question its adequacy and completeness and so on, the fact remains that the designers of computer-chess programs still do not have an acceptable means of estimating the performance of chess programs, without resorting to time-consuming and expensive "matches" against other subjects. Clearly there is considerable scope for improvement, as the success of test sets in related areas like pattern recognition attest.

Here the performance of some contemporary chess program is compared with earlier results from 1981, to help identify the properties of those cases that computers cannot handle well by search alone and to show the relative progress that has been made. Even though use of standard tests is still not widespread, many chess programming groups built such sets and a few have been circulated. One of the earliest was the NY 1924 data set (Marsland and Rushton, 1973) of about 800 positions, later used in a minor way to assess the performance of *Tech* (Gillogly 1978), and to develop evaluation function weighting factors (Marsland 1985). At about the same time Ken Thompson was building far larger test suites (Thompson, 1979) and more recently Dap Hartmann worked with some 63,000 positions to extract knowledge from Grandmaster games (Hartmann, 1987a, b). The Hartmann suite was used to tune the evaluation parameters of such programs as *Phoenix* and *Deep*

*) This paper is a revised and expanded version of T. A. Marsland's (1989) The Bratko-Kopec Test Revisited. *New Directions in Game-Tree Search Workshop* reprints (Ed. T. A. Marsland), pp. 135-139, Edmonton, May 1989.

Thought. When one considers that even 63,000 positions is a minuscule fraction of the estimated 10^{40} unique chess positions, what role can the small set of 24 B-K (Bratko-Kopec) positions play? Aside from being too small, the positions can be criticized because they consider only tactical and pawn lever moves, with many other important ideas and structures not covered. The tactical moves are now thought to be too simple for computers. Importance of pawn moves for high calibre play is brought out by the B-K positions better than by any other test set.

Recognizing the narrow scope of the B-K suite, Jens Nielsen is developing a more sophisticated test with a greater range of features and is using it to estimate the Elo rating of commercial chess computers. Nielsen's (1989) system has many facets, using not only time taken to help measure a program's merit, but also testing the program's ability to reject moves. His system includes tests of endgame play, positional play, tactics and traps. At present some 145 problems are posed from 80 positions (many positions require the generation of a sequence of moves). Even thought the test is time-consuming to apply, more than 40 programs have been tested and their Elo rating estimated with remarkable correlation to other accepted measures (Nielsen, 1989). Like the B-K test and others, this system is of considerable benefit in the development of new chess programs, since it probes for the presence of specific knowledge and for the absence of common conceptual errors.

2. Previous Results

The original paper by Kopec and Bratko (1982) was also criticized for its unrealistic requirement that the program produce an ordered list of up to three choice moves. Although ordering moves is easy for humans, the pruning algorithm in most chess programs precludes consistent generation of such a list. That objection could have been overcome easily had the experiment been run slightly differently: by providing an ordered list of choice moves and rating performance according to the relative strength of the principal move proposed.

The last and final complaint aimed at prepared test sets is that programs can be tuned to perform well on the suite, perhaps at the expense of their overall playing strength. In principle, this objection is valid and serious, but in practice the pawn lever positions in particular have led to an appreciation of the importance of knowledge assessing critical pawn configurations. Also the harder tactical problems led to the development of selective search extensions (Anantharaman, Campbell and Hsu, 1988) to identify and follow forced variations. Further, far more critical to the playing strength of programs than performance on any test suite are other factors, such as good use of time (Hyatt 1984; Anantharaman 1990), and effective use of transportation tables in the endgame (Nelson 1985). Nevertheless, it is clear from the results that the recognized best chess programs exhibit superior performance on the B-K test.

Consider Table 1 (Kopec and Bratko 1982), which shows an extract from the original results. Although the weakest programs fared badly when this test set was sprung upon them, some brute-force programs, notably *Belle, Duchess* and *BCP* did well even by today's standards. In particular, in 1981 *Belle* achieved a score of 18, which today is only exceeded by a handful of programs. Nevertheless, there can be no doubt that the comparably performing programs of today are stronger than *Belle '81*.

Computer Subjects				
Program	Rating	Score	T	L
1. Chess Challenger '10'	Unr	1	1	0
2. Chess Challenger '7'	Unr	5	2	3
3. Sensory Chess Challenger	Unr	5	3	2
4. Sargon 2.5	1720 ~	5	2	3
5. AWIT	1400	5	4	1
6. OSTRICH81	1450 ~	6	4	2
7. CHAOS	1820	6	5	1
8. Chess Champion Mk V (E)	1885 ~	6.83	5	1.83
9. Morphy Encore	1800 ~	9.33	6	3.3
10. BCP	1605 ~	13	10	3
11. DUCHESS	1850	16.50	10.5	6
12. BELLE	2150	18.25	11	7.25

Table 1: An extract from the original (1981)Bratko-Kopec results.

Key: (E) Experimental version; ~ Rating is an estimate; (Unr) Unrated;
(T) Tactical score; (L) Score on pawn lever positions.

Note: Programs running off mainframe computers have names entirely in
upper case letter. Others are stand-alone microcomputer programs.

3. Interpretation of Current Performance

Turning now to the results of eight years later, Table 2 and Table 3, present the data supplied by applicants to the 6th World Computer Chess Championships, plus some 1986 data for *Awit*'83. Of the twelve tactical postitions, Table 2, about half the programs can solve nearly all (thus equaling the *Belle* '81 score). Further, virtually all the programs can solve far more than half the tactical positions. As these results show, the harder problems are positions 10 and 22, which are presented in Figure 1.

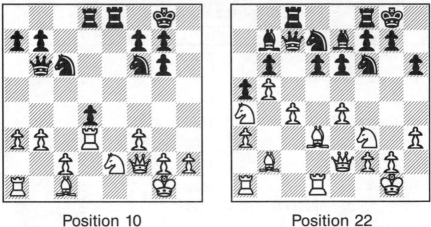

Position 10
Black plays ... Ne5

Position 22
Black plays ... Bxe4

Figure 1: Two difficult tactical positions.

However, there was no pattern to explain why the eight programs which successfully solved 11 tactical problems could not solve them all, since their failures were uniformly distributed across five different problems (positions 7, 10, 16, 18 and 22). Also, there can be little doubt that these top programs could be "tuned" to solve all twelve B-K tactical problems, but at what cost to their average playing strength? Equally it would seem that problems 1, 12, 14, 15, 16, 19 and 21 are within reach of solution by all contemporary programs, given enough effort. So in some sense those positions are a measure of minimal acceptable strength.

For the lever positions shown in Table 3, however, few programs can solve more than half, and only three positions can be solved by almost all the programs. In particular, problems 4, 5, and 8 seem easy enough for those programs that have the right knowledge. Interestingly, 13 of the 22 programs solved all three problems and the others only failed to solve one each! On the other hand, almost no program can solve the three most difficult (namely positions 2, 9 and 23), all of which involve a pawn sacrifice for positional gain, either specifically, or as part of the analysis of the principal variations. Figure 2 shows two representative positions. Not only are these problems difficult, but also it is possible that the few programs which were successful in solving them may just have been lucky. Even so, there are possibilities for improvement, since although 15 programs solved neither problem 9 nor 23, *Mephisto* was able to solve both! This suggests that *Mephisto* might contain special pawn knowledge not found in other programs.

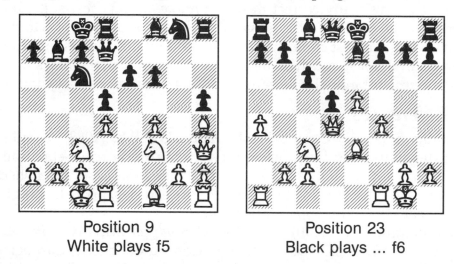

Position 9	Position 23
White plays f5	Black plays ... f6

Figure 2: Two difficult pawn lever positions.

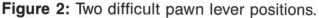

4. Interpretation of Current Performance

Our data leads to the final questions: Is the B-K test good enough for estimating the performance of chess programs? Clearly not, since the suite is too small and not wide-ranging enough. Despite that shortcoming, are there still things for programmers to learn from the B-K test? Clearly yes, especially for new programs and those programs which are alone in failing to solve a particular problem. Conversely, when several programs solve one problem, some programming error or lack of knowledge is preventing correct solution by the others. Finally, although more and more chess programs are incorporating selective extensions and dynamic width control in the deeper portions of the search, the results show that at least one fully selective search program, Awit'83, achieved a respectable score on the test suite even though it was selective at every level in its search, and even though in over-the-board play it had a checkered career. This suggests that in the middle game one can do quite well with selective search, but in the end game totally different knowledge, time control and more dynamic search-depth limits are required. Lack of these features accounted for Awit's relatively poorer endgame play.

To conclude, the data presented here provides an opportunity to consider whether the calibre of a chess program is measured not so much by how many correct moves it makes in any test suite, but rather by the quality of the moves it proposes as alternatives to the acknowledged best choices. That is, the quality of a chess program is measured not so much by the frequency with which it plays optimal moves, but more by the strength of its less than perfect choices.

4. References

Anantharaman, T., Campbell, M.S. and Hsu, F-h. (1988) Singular Extensions: Adding Selectivity to Brute-Force Searching. *ICCA Journal*, Vol. 11, No. 4, pp. 135-143. Also published (1988) in AAAI Spring Symposium Proceedings, pp. 8-13, and to appear (1990) in *Artificial Intelligence*.

Anantharaman, T. (1990). *A Statistical Study of Selective Min-Max Search*. Ph.D. thesis, Department of Computer Science, Carnegie-Mellon University, in preparation.

Gillogly, J. J. (1978). *Performance Analysis of the Technology Chess Program*. Ph.D. thesis, Department of Computer Science, Carnegie-Mellon University.

Hartmann, D. (1987). How To Extract Relevant Knowledge From Grandmaster Games, Part 1. *ICCA Journal*, Vol. 10, No. 1, pp. 14-36.

Hyatt, R. M. (1984). Using Time Wisely. *ICCA Journal*, Vol. 7, No. 1, pp. 4-9

Kopec, D. and Bratko, I. (1982). The Bratko-Kopec Experiment: A Comparison of Human and Computer Performance. *Advances in Computer Chess 3* (Ed. M. R. B. Clarke), pp. 57-72, Pergamon Press.

Marsland, T. A. and Rushton, P. (1973) Mechanisms for Comparing Chess Programs. *Proceedings ACM National Conference*, Oct., pp 202-205.

Marsland, T. A. (1985). Evaluation-Function Factors. *ICCA Journal*, Vol. 8, No. 2, pp. 47-57.

Nelson, H. L. (1985). Hash Tables in Cray Blitz. ICCA Journal, Vol. 8, No. 1, pp. 3-13.

Nielsen, J. B. (1989). Private Communication, August.

Reinfeld, F. (1945). *Win At Chess*, McKay, New York. Also (1958), Dover, New York.

Thompson, K. (1979). Private Communication, Bell Laboratories, N.J.

Appendix

Below the 1989 Bratko-Kopec results for the tactical positions (Table 2) as well as the 1989 Bratko Kopec results for the lever positions (Table 3) are presented.

Position Tactical (T)	1 Qd1	5 Nd5	7 Nf6	10 Ne5	12 Bf5	14 Qd2	15 Qxg7	16 Ne4	18 Nb3	19 Rxe4	21 Nh6	22 Bxe4	Ttl
Al Chess	ok	ok	ok	ok	ok	ok	ok	ok	ok	ok	ok	ok	12
Awit'83	ok	ok	Bd6	Qc5	ok	ok	ok	ok	ok	ok	ok	c5	9
Bebe	ok	ok	ok	Rd7	ok	ok	ok	ok	ok	ok	ok	ok	11
BP	ok	ok	Rg3	Qc5	ok	ok	ok	ok	ok	ok	ok	Nh5	9
Centaur	ok	e5	ok	Qc5	ok	ok	ok	ok	e5	ok	ok	e5	9
Cray Blitz	ok	ok	ok	ok	ok	ok	ok	ok	ok	ok	ok	ok	12
Dappet	ok	Bf4	ok	Wc5	ok	ok	ok	ok	e5	ok	ok	e5	8
Deep Thought	ok	ok	ok	ok	ok	ok	ok	Qh5	ok	ok	ok	ok	11
Hitech	ok	ok	Ra2	ok	ok	ok	ok	ok	f5	ok	ok	ok	11
Lachex	ok	ok	ok	ok	ok	ok	ok	ok	f5	ok	ok	ok	11
Mach 4	ok	ok	ok	ok	ok	ok	ok	ok	ok	ok	ok	ok	11
Mephisto	ok	ok	Qc1	Qc5	ok	ok	ok	Be6	ok	ok	ok	Ne5	11
Merlin	ok	ok	ok	ok	ok	ok	ok	Be6	ok	ok	ok	Ne5	10
Modul	ok	ok	ok	ok	ok	ok	ok	ok	ok	ok	ok	ok	12
Much	ok	Bf4	ok	Qc7	ok	ok	ok	ok	bg4	ok	ok	Rd8	8
Pandix	ok	Rad1	Rg3	Qc5	ok	ok	ok	ok	Qb6	ok	ok	ok	7
Phoenix	ok	ok	ok	ok	ok	ok	ok	ok	Qb6	ok	ok	ok	11
Rebel	ok	ok	ok	ok	ok	ok	ok	ok	ok	ok	ok	Ne5	11
Shess	ok	Rad1	Bb4	Qc5	ok	ok	ok	Be7	Bg4	ok	Qe3	Ne5	5
Waycool	ok	ok	Ra2	ok	ok	ok	ok	ok	ok	ok	ok	Nh5	10
Y!89	ok	ok	Bb4	ok	ok	ok	ok	ok	Qb6	ok	ok	e5	9
Zarkov	ok	ok	ok	Qc5	ok	ok	ok	ok	f5	ok	ok	Rd8	9

Table 2: Results for the B-K tactical positions.

Position Lever (L)	2	3	4	6	8	9	11	13	17	20	23	24	Ttl
	d5	f5	e6	g6	f5	f5	f4	b4	h5	g4	f6	f4	12
Al Chess	e5	ok	ok	ok	ok	Re1	ok	ok	h6	Kb1	Bf5	ok	6
Awit'83	Rb1	a5	ok	ok	ok	Re1	ok	Rac1	e6	Qh5	Bf5	ok	7
Bebe	Ke3	f5	ok	Kg4	Nc3	Rc1	ok	ok	ok	Kb1	Bf5	b:c5	6
BP	e5	Qd8	ok	ok	ok	Bb5	Rfb1	Rac1	ok	Nb5	Bf5	ok	5
Centaur	e5	Qc7	ok	C4	ok	Re1	Nf5	Rac1	Qc8	Nc5	Bf5	e:f5	2
Cray Blitz	g5	ok	ok	ok	ok	Bd3	ok	ok	c6	ok	o-o	ok	8
Dappet	e5	ok	ok	ok	e5	ok	ok	ok	h6	Nb5	Bf5	ok	6
Deep Thought	Kf3	Qd8	ok	ok	f6	Bb5	ok	ok	c6	a3	Bf5	ok	6
Hitech	f5	Bd8	ok	ok	ok	Re1	Nf5	ok	ok	ok	Bf5	e:f5	5
Lachex	e3	Rg8	ok	ok	ok	Bd3	ok	ok	a5	ok	Bf5	ok	6
Mach 4	Kf3	Rd8	ok	ok	ok	Re1	Nf5	ok	c6	Kb1	Bf5	e:f5	4
Mephisto	Kf3	Bd8	ok	ok	ok	ok	Nf5	ok	c6	c5	Bf5	ok	7
Merlin	Kf3	ok	Nf3	ok	ok	g3	Nf5	ok	ok	Nb5	Bf5	ok	6
Modul	Kf3	Bd8	ok	ok	ok	g3	ok	ok	c5	ok	Bf5	ok	5
Much	e5	Rd8	ok	Kf3	ok	g3	Qa2	Rac1	Nb8	Nb5	Bf5	b:c5	2
Pandix	Kf3	Qd8	ok	ok	ok	Re1	ok	ok	c6	Qb5	Bf5	ok	6
Phoenix	Kf3	ok	ok	Kg4	ok	Re1	ok	ok	c6	Qh5	Bf5	ok	6
Rebel	Kf3	Bd8	ok	ok	ok	Re1	ok	ok	c6	ok	Bf5	ok	7
Shess	e5	ok	ok	ok	h4	Re1	ok	ok	b6	Nb5	Bf5	b:c5	5
Waycool	f5	ok	ok	a4	ok	ok	ok	Qe2	b6	Nb5	Bf5	f5	5
Y!89	e5	ok	ok	ok	ok	Bb5	Rfb1	b3	h6	Qh5	Bf5	e:f5	3
Zarkov	e5	ok	ok	ok	ok	ok	ok	ok	h6	h3	Bf5	e:f5	6

Table 3: Results for the B-K lever positions.

Appendix 2

Comparison and Testing of Commercial Computer Chess Programs

By Shawn Benn and Danny Kopec

In 1992 Shawn Benn, an undergraduate computer science student in co-author D. Kopec's artificial intelligence class at the University of Maine and later a graduate student in computer science, continued experiments in evaluating computer chess programs using the Bratko-Kopec Test. He tested six commercial computer chess programs and his results were presented at the World Microcomputer Chess Championship in Madrid, Spain in November, 1992 (Comparison and Testing of Six Commercial Computer Chess Programs, Benn and Kopec, 1992). This paper was published in a significantly abridged form as "The Bratko-Kopec Test Recalibrated" (*ICCA Journal*, Vol. 16 No. 3, pp. 144-46, September, 1993). Here we present the main results of that study and some more recent evaluations of two popular commercial programs by Mr. Benn.

The six programs tested were: THE CHESSMASTER 3000 (CM3000), EXCEL 68000 (stand-alone), M CHESS, SARGON IV, SARGON V, and ZARKOV 2.5. CM3000, M CHESS, SARGON V and ZARKOV 2.5. They were tested on an 80386 microprocessor with a speed of 33 Megahertz.

CM3000 is distributed by Software Toolworks, Inc. It is the successor to CHESSMASTER 2100 which had a rating of about 2100. CM3000 was tested using an IBM compatible computer and was manufactured in 1991.

The EXCEL 68000 runs as a stand-alone unit. It runs on a 68000 microprocessor running at 12 megahertz. It was manufactured by Fidelity International of Miami, Florida.

M CHESS was written and distributed by Martin Hirsch in 1991. It was tested on an IBM compatible computer.

SARGON IV was tested on a Macintosh. It was published by Spinnaker Software of Cambridge, Massachusetts. It was released in 1988. Its authors are Dan and Kathe Spracklen.

SARGON V was developed by Activision of Palo Alto, California in December, 1991 and was a completely revised production of SARGON IV with many new added features. It was tested on an IBM-compatible computer. The program version evaluated by Benn was a Beta version just before its release in final form. The authors of Sargon V's chess engine are Dan and Kathe Spracklen, with a number of contributors to the overall project.

The last computer chess program tested was ZARKOV 2.5. It was developed by John Stanbeck in 1991 and was distributed by Chess Laboratories of Pasadena, California. It was also tested on an IBM-compatible computer.

The method used to test the six programs is as follows: 1 point was given to the program if it found the best move at two minutes, 1/2 point was given if the program found the best move at one-and-a-half minutes, 1/3 of a point if the program found the best move at one minute, and 1/4 of a point if the program found the best move at 30 seconds. The move at two minutes is to correlate to the subject's best move choice. The move at one-and-a-half minutes correlates to the second-best move choice and so on. Each position was posed as a problem for each of the six programs. Each program was given two minutes to choose a best move. The move selected at each time interval was recorded. Results with each program are shown on the following page.

Table 1
Move Choice at Two Minute Mark

Position	Type	Best Move(s)	CM-3000	Excel 68000	M Chess	Sargon IV	Sargon V	Zarkov 2.5
1	T	...Qd1 +	...Qd1 +	...Qd1 +	...Qd1 +	...Qd1 +	...Qd1 +	...Qd1 +
2	L	d5	e5	Ke3	Ra1	Kf3	Ke2	e5
3	L	... f5	... f5	Rg8	Qd8	Rg8	Rg8	Qd8
4	L	e6	e6	Nf3	e6	Nf3	Nf3	e6
5	T	Nd5, a4	Rd1	Nd5	Nd5	Bf4	a4	Nd5
6	L	g6	Kg4	g6	Kg4	g6	g6	Kg4
7	T	Nf6	Bb4	Bd6	Nf6	Bb4	Nf6	Nf6
8	L	f5	Kd2	f5	f5	f5	f5	f5
9	L	f5	Re1	Bb5	Re1	Re1	Re1	Re1
10	T	... Ne5	Qc5	Qc5	... Ne5	Qc5	Qc5	... Ne5
11	L	f4	Nf5	Nf5	f4	Nf5	Nf5	f4
12	T	... Bf5	... Bf5	... Bf5	... Bf5	... Bf5	... Bf5	... Bf5
13	L	b4	b3	b4	Rc1	b4	b4	Rc1
14	T	Qd2, Qe1	Qd2	Qd2	Qd2	Qe1	Qd2	Qd2
15	T	Qxg7 +	Qxg7 +	Qxg7 +	Qxg7 +	Qxg7 +	Qxg7 +	Qxg7 +
16	T	Ne4	Ne4	Ne4	Ne4	Ne4	Ne4	Ne4
17	L	... h5	... h5	... h5	a5	... h5	... h5	h6
18	T	... Nb3	... Nb3	Qb6	... Nb3	Qb6	... Nb3	Bg4
19	T	... Rxe4	... Rxe4	... Rxe4	... Rxe4	... Rxe4	... Rxe4	... Rxe4
20	L	g4	g4	Qh5	h3	h3	h3	Nb5
21	T	Nh6	Nh6	Nh6	Nh6	Nh6	Nh6	Nh6
22	T	... Bxe4	Re8	Ne5	... Bxe4	Ne5	Ne5	Nh5
23	L	... f6	Bf5	Bf5	Bf5	Bf5	Bf5	Bf5
24	L	f4	f4	exf5	exf5	exf5	exf5	exf5
		Score:	13.00	12.25	15.00	11.00	14.00	13.00

CM3000 = The Chessmaster 3000

All the programs tested have the feature of a search window. Having this feature made it unnecessary to have the program actually play a move. This was because the search window lets the user see which move the program thinks is the best move to play. Without the search window, one would have to force a move and retract it and restart the time. The search window feature saved much time in implementing and completing the test set.

All six programs scored fairly highly. M CHESS scored the highest with fifteen points.

The following chart based on previous results with the Bratko-Kopec Test was used to estimate the rating of each program:

Table 2
Rating/Score Equivalencies

Rating	Score
1300-1599	0-4
1600-1799	5-6
1800-1999	7-8
2000-2199	09-12
2200-2399	13-16
2400 +	17-24

Source: Kopec, Newborn, Yu, 1986,
reprinted in this work as Appendix 1.

The next chart shows the total scores and estimated ratings for each of the programs. It may be concluded from the range of scores (11-15) that the programs are fairly close in overall strength. Furthermore, these scores give credence to the claim that the programs' strengths lie between 2100 and 2300.

Table 3
Estimated Ratings of Six Programs

Program	Rating*	Score	Tactical	Lever	12(T-L)/S
M Chess	2300	15.00	12	3.00	7.20
Sargon V	2250	14.00	10	4.00	5.14
Zarkov 2.5	2200	13.00	10	3.00	6.46
Chessmaster 3000	2200	13.00	8	5.00	2.77
Excel 68000	2150	12.25	8	4.25	3.67
Sargon IV	2100	11.00	7	4.00	3.27

* Estimate based on previous tests using Bratko-Kopec Set on computer programs

The results of the test set on each of the programs demonstrated the characteristics of each program. All the programs fared a lot better on the tactical positions than they did on the lever positions. This was also a conclusion from the original Bratko-Kopec Experiment. More research effort should concentrate on knowledge-based concepts like levers in chess.

For more details about the Bratko-Kopec Test and the meaning of scores on it, see Chapter 1 in this volume or the original paper by Bratko and Kopec published in *Advances in Computer Chess 3*, (ed. M.R.B. Clarke, 1982).

In January, 1995, Mr. Benn tested the programs Fritz3 and Chessmaster 4000 which have scored 18.0 and 18.25 respectively on the Bratko-Kopec Test. These scores correspond to the 2300+ USCF rating range, which may indeed be the actual strength of Fritz3 and Chessmaster 4000. They represent significant improvements over the six commercial programs Mr. Benn tested earlier which had scored in the 11-15 range. Nontheless, the program BELLE had scored 18.0 on this test set (with a similar lever/tactics breakdown) as early as 1983.

Table 4
Results of Fritz3 on Bratko-Kopec Test

Position	Type/ To move	Best Move	0:30	1:00	1:30	2:00	Pts
1	T Black	...Qd1+	...Qd1+	...Qd1+	...Qd1+	...Qd1+	1
2	L White	d5	f3	f5	g2	g2	0
3	L Black	... f5	... f5	... f5	... f5	... f5	1
4	L White	e6	e6	e6	e6	e6	1
5	T White	Nd5, a4	Rd1	Nd5	Nd5	Nd5	1
6	L White	g6	g6	g6	g6	g6	1
7	T White	Nf6	Nf6	Nf6	Nf6	Nf6	1
8	L White	f5	f5	f5	f5	f5	1
9	L White	f5	g3	g3	g3	g3	0
10	T Black	... Ne5	... Ne5	... Ne5	... Ne5	... Ne5	1
11	L White	f4	Rb1	Rb1	Rb1	Rb1	1
12	T Black	... Bf5	... Bf5	... Bf5	... Bf5	... Bf5	1
13	L White	b4	b4	b4	b4	b4	1
14	T White	Qd2*	Qd2	Qd2	Qd2	Qd2	1
15	T White	Qxg7+	Qxg7+	Qxg7+	Qxg7+	Qxg7+	1
16	T White	Ne4	Ne4	Ne4	Ne4	Ne4	1
17	L Black	... h5	... h6	... h6	... h6	... h6	0
18	T Black	... Nb3	... Nb3	... Nb3	... Nb3	... Nb3	1
19	T Black	... Rxe4	... Rxe4	... Rxe4	... Rxe4	... Rxe4	1
20	L White	g4	Nb5	h3	h3	h3	0
21	T White	Nh6	Nh6	Nh6	Nh6	Nh6	1
22	T Black	... Bxe4	... Bxe4	... Bxe4	... Bxe4	... Bxe4	1
23	L Black	... f6	... Bf5	... f6	... f6	... f6	1
24	L White	f4	f3	f3	f3	f3	0

Table 5
Total Scores for Fritz3

	Possible Points	Scored Points
Tactical	12	12
Lever	12	6
Total	24	18

Testing performed by Shawn Benn, 1995.

Table 6
Results of Chessmaster 4000 on Bratko-Kopec Test

Position	Type/ To move	Best Move	0:30	1:00	1:30	2:00	Pts
1	T Black	...Qd1+	...Qd1+	...Qd1+	...Qd1+	...Qd1+	1
2	L White	d5	Kf3	Kf3	g5	g5	0
3	L Black	... f5	... f5	... Kg8	... Kg8	... Kg8	.25
4	L White	e6	e6	e6	e6	e6	1
5	T White	Nd5, a4	a4	a4	a4	Nd5	1
6	L White	g6	g6	g6	g6	g6	1
7	T White	Nf6	Nf6	Nf6	Nf6	Nf6	1
8	L White	f5	f5	f5	f5	f5	1
9	L White	f5	Re1	Re1	Bd3	Bd3	0
10	T Black	... Ne5	... Qc5	... Ne5	... Ne5	... Ne5	1
11	L White	f4	f4	f4	f4	f4	1
12	T Black	... Bf5	... Bf5	... Bf5	... Bf5	... Bf5	1
13	L White	b4	e5	b4	b4	b4	1
14	T White	Qd2*	Qd2	Qd2	Qd2	Qd2	1
15	T White	Qxg7+	Qxg7+	Qxg7+	Qxg7+	Qxg7+	1
16	T White	Ne4	Ne4	Ne4	Ne4	Ne4	1
17	L Black	... h5	... c5	... c5	... c5	... Ne8	0
18	T Black	... Nb3	... Nb3	... Nb3	... Nb3	... Nb3	1
19	T Black	... Rxe4	... Rxe4	... Rxe4	... Rxe4	... Rxe4	1
20	L White	g4	Nb5	Nb5	Nb5	Nb5	0
21	T White	Nh6	Nh6	Nh6	Nh6	Nh6	1
22	T Black	... Bxe4	... Bxe4	... Bxe4	... Bxe4	... Bxe4	1
23	L Black	... f6	... Bf5	... Bf5	... Bf5	... Bf5	0
24	L White	f4	f4	f4	f4	f4	1

Table 7
Total Scores for Chessmaster 4000

	Possible Points	Scored Points
Tactical	12	12.00
Lever	12	6.25
Total	24	18.25

Testing performed by Shawn Benn, 1995.

Appendix 3

Camp Test 1995 Results

The table below represents the results of nine subjects on the Camptest administered to the top ("A") group at Kopec's Chess Camp (July 23-30) in 1995. This was quite a strong group, averaging 1948 across subjects ranging from ages 14 to 47. It should be mentioned that this test set has 17 T (tactical) positions and 7 L (lever) positions, with the T positions predominating slightly as in earlier test sets, i.e. an average score of 9.22 from 17 is a better result than an average of 3.02 from 7. In this set of 24 positions, there are eight opening, eight middle-game, and eight endgame test positions. Average results show that subjects could get the answers to about 50% of the O and M positions correctly. However with the eight endgame examples, subjects were able to score better (avg. 5.1) than they had on average in opening (3.7) and middlegame (3.45) positions.

The results of the test administered to this small but rather uniform group of subjects are compelling. Overall total scores are a little higher than on previous tests we have administered despite the perceived difficulty of the test. This may be primarily due to T scores, ranging from 7 to 12 — a higher percentage is enabled by the existence of more T positions in the test set (17 rather than 12 as in the past). A factor in the relatively high average scores on endgame positions may be that endgame positions have fewer reasonable choices of best move, thereby enabling more partial credit.

Name	Age	Country	Rating	T	L	O	M	E	Total
Aaron Lewis	16	US	1956	6.93	1.58	1.30	2.58	4.58	8.50
Judah Ash	47	US	2000	7.33	2.33	3.00	3.00	3.66	9.66
Jim Takagi	35	US	1763	7.83	2.33	2.50	3.50	4.17	10.16
Barry Petersen	43	US	1980	9.00	1.83	4.30	1.83	4.66	10.83
Patrick Hummel	10	US	1900	9.58	3.25	5.50	2.00	5.33	12.83
Bob Boylan	45	US	1900	10.75	2.50	3.80	3.50	6.00	13.25
Emmanuel Amigues	15	France	2116	7.83	6.00	2.70	5.50	5.66	13.83
Tom Hirsch	36	US	1809	11.50	3.50	4.00	5.50	5.50	15.00
Victor Ying	14	US/China	2108	12.25	3.83	6.00	3.70	6.33	16.08
		Average	1948	9.22	3.02	3.70	3.46	5.10	12.71

Appendix 4

Novtest Scores from Kopec's Chess Camp 1995

Results on the Novtest administered at Kopec's Chess Camp in 1995 indicate that the test was very effective in serving its purpose: to determine what conceptual knowledge is lacking in players who would score very poorly on other tests. Subjects who scored better than 50% (12 or higher) were for the most part rated over 1100. The test helps us to determine what instruction areas novices should focus on.

Name	Score	10/95 Rating	12/95 Rating
Geoff Polizoti	23	1522	1593
Josh Friedel	22	1517	1639
Andrew Hellenschmidt	21	1501	1570
Jeremy Kallen	20	1609/18	—
Evan Sonkin	19	1381	1448
Yuri Cantor	18	1381/13	1418/17
Tim Garrett	17	1288	1335
Robbie Title	17	1127	1106
Igor Petrakov	17	983	—
Elan Rodan	16	1340/12	—
Jason Power	16	1167	—
Taylor Curtis	16	1258	—
Ian Mangion	16	1401	—
Willy Weddig	15	1251	—
Chris Williams	15	1196	1198
Justin Smith	14	946	1007
Alexander Wong	14	1202/4	—
Brett Koonce	13	1299/4	—
David Byowitz	12	—	965
Matthew Blaine	12	621/4	—
Kris Hibbett	11	—	1224
Ben Hardy	11	1079/4	—
David Koonce	11	—	—
Michael Lazarus	11	—	1170/4
Greg Erhardt	10	—	—
Ian MacKenzie	10	984/4	1144/8
Paul Mastrangeli	9	—	—
Adam Marianacci	8	—	1101
Geoff Newcombe	7	1084	—
Ethan Lippett	7	—	—
Amal Vajda	6	—	—

"—" indicates that the subject had no published rating in the relevant rating list.

Introduction to Appendices 5, 6, 7, 8 and 9 (New Edition)

Recall that the continuing goal of this work reported in this book has been to develop a reliable method of evaluating chess strength based on the knowledge that is deemed necessary to find the correct move(s) in a position. In this way we have attempted to exemplify the knowledge and thinking which distinguishes Chess as indeed *The Royal Game*. Due to game speedup, many players (especially young ones) have no sense of the kind of depth and beauty may be hidden in chess thinking and analysis. It is quite likely that most young players (say under age 20) are unable to make the distinction between the kind of thinking and analysis which can go into Correspondence Chess (at three days a move) and fast forms of chess (say under 45 minutes each).

What follows is also new material since the publication of the original volume, *Test, Evaluate, and Improve Your Chess: a knowledge-based approach* (with Hal Terrie, Hypermodern Press, San Francisco, July, 1997). In 1976 the publisher of that book, FM Jim Eade, participated in a class with Danny Kopec whereby he learned the key concepts which are tested in the Bratko-Kopec Test. His game improved so markedly after taking the test and its review that he felt compelled to publish the book.

The tests we have developed, described, and employed in this book have proven to be very valuable instructional tools. They cover all parts of the game of chess and offer something for everyone. The post mortem analysis of subjects' performance on the tests has also been extremely valuable. Overall they provide the basis of a curriculum for chess instruction.

Hence in addition to the updated and revised material (including Chapter 6: The Intermediate Test) which we have added to the main body of the book, we have added:

Appendix 5: Novtest Scores from Kopec's Chess Camp 2001

Appendix 6: Performance Analysis of single and multiprocessor CRAFTY on Various Compilers

Appendix 7: Some Additional Results With Human Subjects (Camptest 1995)

Appendix 8: Miscellaneous Results with Bratko - Kopec Test (32 Subjects) Analysis of Within-Position Test Results

Appendix 9: Rating Improvement with Testing

Appendix 5

Novtest Scores from Kopec's Chess Camp 2001

New results from the most recent Novtest administered at Kopec's Chess Camp in 2001 indicate that the test is still performing its job effectively: helping us to assign campers to appropriate instruction groups. Those who scored well above what their ratings would predict were placed in more advanced groups. For the most part, the rating/score equivalence table continues to hold up — it usually takes a rating of 1100 or better to score over 50% (12 correct).

Name	Score	08/01 Rating
Daniel Copeland	20	1378
Cayley Robinson	19	1359
Rafael Witten	17	1289
Daniel Erenrich	17	1122
Palmer Mebane	14	1208
Evan Clark	13	769
Robbie Boettger	12	842
Lucien Taillac	11	777
Benjamin Phillips	11	620
Jared Littlefield	9	1163
Chapman Thomas	9	112
Eric Bachrach	8	571
Rohith Pottabathni	7	607
Nicholas Gosselin	6	643
Edward Barba	5	587

The significance of these tests (Novtest, Intermediate, and in fact all of our tests) is not so much how well they reflect chess ability, but more so in how they help instructors (and students) learn to focus their teaching and study.

Appendix 6

Performance Analysis of single and multiprocessor CRAFTY on Various Compilers

Backgound

The work reported here has its roots in a paper presented and published in 1990 entitled "A Taxonomy of Chess Concepts" (Berliner, Kopec, & Northam, 1990) and later a slightly revised version appeared in Berliner, Kopec, and Northham, (1991). The goal of that research was to demonstrate that the problem-space of chess positions can be broken down into well-defined patterns which can be easily classified and labeled. It has generally been accepted that such patterns are the basis for strong chess play. Although very strong (close to world championship caliber) chess play has been largely accomplished by brute force methods, it is our belief that there will always be a domain space in the game of chess which will elude mastery and may require specialist knowledge, particularly in endings (ibid). That work also addressed the concept of "Performance vs. Competence," which is essentially the distinction between "weak AI and strong AI." Performance of computer programs in computationally tasking domains may be impressive despite a lack or knowledge or understanding of the domain. Competence, akin to strong AI, is usually based on domain-specific knowledge with AI methods employed to solve challenging problems. In the sections which follow, the performance of the chess program CRAFTY, the strongest open-source chess program is analyzed running on the GCC.

Our effort to obtain a better understanding of the essential building blocks of chess knowledge and how they relate to chess play at diverse levels, continues.

The Bratko-Kopec Test (See Chapter 1)

The first test, The Bratko-Kopec Test (BKTEST) (Kopec & Bratko, 1982), was designed with the purpose of distinguishing between intermediate and advanced chess playing strength with two concepts in mind: tactics and levers. Over the years this test has proven extremely reliable in distinguishing between chessplayer rating levels for both man and machine, and has therefore proven to be by far our most popular test. It demonstrated that intermediate level chess play is dominated by the ability to play reasonable tactics, but the knowledge of levers, a quasitactical and positional type of pawn move offering a trade of pawns (a lever is a pawn move which by our definition either improves your pawn structure and/or damages your opponent's pawn structure) is an example of an important strategic chess concept which may distinguish higher level play from intermediate level play.

Performance results of CRAFTY on the BKTEST using Compaq's CXX compiler and Gnu C (GCC) compilers was quite strong and comparable. Tested for solutions at 30 sec, 1 minute, 1.5 minutes, and 2 minutes, CXX scored 19 correct on the test and GCC scored 18. CXX's overall score of 19/24 in this testing was to be expected. For many years programmers have been tweaking their programs to this test. The search depth was about 12 ply on all time intervals. A score of 19 on this test is indicative of a 2400+ ELO rated program.

The positions mishandled by CXX were numbers 3, 9, 17, 23, and 24 with difficulty levels 3, 2, 2, 4 and 2 respectively (where 1 is low and 4 is high). This is consistent with earlier results (see Appendix 1-c, by Professor T. A. Marsland. These are all "L" or lever positions requiring domainspecific knowledge. This is a part of chess play where continuous improvements to CRAFTY have been made, but which still remains a relative weakness.

The New Positions Test (See Chapter 1)

In early work (Kopec, Newborn and Wu, 1983) the purpose of one of our studies was to evaluate "Are Two Heads Better Than One?" both in terms of human, and later, computer performance in chess problems. In order to do this effectively we needed a test similar to the BKTEST, so that we could evaluate performance by subjects working alone and in pairs. Again this test has 12 lever positions and 12 tactical positions. Here CRAFTY CXX scores 13/24 with two minutes and one and a half minutes per position. At one minute, and at 30 seconds per position CXX scored 12/24. The performance of the GCC Compiler on this test suite is essentially identical to that of CXX. The average search depth of both compilers over the four time intervals tested was over 12 ply.

Of the 11 positions which CRAFTY failed to get the correct answer, eight were lever type positions. The average difficulty level of the positions where CRAFTY failed to find the correct move was just under 3. For the three tactical (T) positions missed the difficulty levels were 3, 4, and 4 respectively. Clearly CRAFTY is still needs considerable work in the area of levers (positional play). The L positions CRAFTY misses are at all levels. Its choices in these positions were not particularly impressive.

The Camp Test (1995) (See Chapter 2)

The Camp Test was specifically designed to be more difficult than the BKTest or the New Positions Test. The main idea behind this test is that levers vs. tactics should no longer be the main distinguishing feature, but that the performance in the three phases of chess play will also be tested. Hence there are eight opening positions, eight middlegame positions, and eight endings. There are also T and L positions. Here CXX's overall score of 10 right at two minutes and one and a half minutes, and 11 right at one minute and at 30 seconds, is slightly puzzling. One explanation may be that sometimes cutoffs of variations can occur at deeper search depths, affecting move choices. GCC does very slightly worse, scoring 10 for two minutes and one and a half minutes, and at 30 seconds, and 11 for one minute.

The average search depth for both compilers is over 13. This greater score can be explained by the fact that the test contains more endgame positions than the previous two tests. With reduced material programs are able to search more deeply.

CRAFTY's poor performance on this test can be attributed to its performance on the eight endgame positions (getting seven of them wrong). All of the program's errors in the endgame positions indicate that it needs a lot of special purpose knowledge about the endgame (Bratko, Kopec, Michie, 1978). This is precisely the reason why these positions were selected for this test suite. In addition, the three middlegame positions missed are all of a lever nature, consistent with earlier performance. Finally, the 4 opening positions (specifically chosen for their theoretical nature) need mention. In each case the program chooses an inferior move. One such position (#3) is solved in one minute, and in 30 seconds, but not in one and a half minutes or two minutes.

The Rook and Pawn Endings Test

For this test the program, considering its poor endgame display in the previous test, does fairly well, scoring 21, 19, 18 and 19 correct, respectively, for two minutes, one and a half minutes, one minute, and at 30 seconds over 35 positions in total. GCC scored significantly less well (19, 18, 15, 18 respectively, or 10.0% lower) on these four time frames of testing. On the one minute time frame CXX searched 42.7% more nodes and scored 20% better. Generally, both compilers averaged a search depth of about 14 ply.

The Other Endings Test

Both compilers' performances on this test was impressive. CXX scored 20, 20, 21, 21, (out of a possible maxium of 27) over two minutes, one and a half minutes, one minute, and at 30 seconds respectively and GCC scored 21 across the board. Average search depth was nearly 15 ply for both compilers, although GCC searched about 5% fewer nodes. We would like to acknowledge NM Jim Boray, a manager at the Compaq Corporation. Without his support the research reported in this Appendix would not have been possible.

Appendix 7

Some Results with Human Subjects

Camp Test 1995
Administered in 2001

Ratings	Name/Links	1	2	3	4	5	6	7	8	9	10	11
812	Danny Tashjian	1	0	0	1	1	0	1	1	0	0	0
1197	Eugene Bogulslavskiy	0	1	0	0	1	0	1	0	0	0	0
1045	James Habboush	1	$1/4$	0	0	1	0	0	0	0	0	0
1850	Jeremy Hummer	$1/3$	0	$1/2$	0	0	0	0	0	0	0	$1/3$
843	John Rosenberg	1	1	0	0	0	0	0	0	1	0	0
992	Michael Szczepanski	0	0	0	0	1	0	$1/2$	1	0	0	0
1600	Paul Howard	$1/2$	$1/2$	0	0	0	0	$1/3$	0	0	0	0
2007	Ryan Milisits	0	1	1	0	1	1	1	$1/3$	1	$1/2$	1

Average per Question (in decimal)	0.48	0.47	0.19	0.13	0.63	0.13	0.48	0.29	0.25	0.06	0.17

12	13	14	15	16	17	18	19	20	21	22	23	24	Total Correct	Total Wrong	Total Score
0	0	0	$1/2$	1	$1/2$	0	0	$1/2$	0	1	0	0	10	14	$8^1/2$
0	0	0	0	0	0	0	0	1	1	0	0	0	5	19	5
0	0	$1/2$	0	0	0	0	0	$1/2$	0	0	0	0	5	19	$3^1/4$
0	0	$1/4$	0	1	1	0	0	$1/3$	0	$1/2$	0	$1/4$	9	15	$4^1/2$
$1/4$	0	0	0	1	1	0	0	0	$1/2$	1	0	0	8	16	$6^3/4$
0	0	1	0	0	0	0	1	0	0	1	0	0	6	18	$5^1/2$
0	0	0	0	0	1	$1/4$	0	0	1	$1/2$	0	0	7	17	4
$1/2$	0	$1/3$	1	0	1	0	0	$1/4$	1	1	0	0	16	8	13

0.09	0.00	0.26	0.19	0.38	0.56	0.03	0.13	0.32	0.44	0.63	0.00	0.03

The above data for eight human subjects attending Kopec's Chess Camp was collected in July, 2001. It confirms that the Camp Test 1995 is quite hard and it requires at least an expert-level player to score over 10 on this test.

Appendix 8
Miscellaneous Results with Bratko - Kopec Test (32 Subjects)Analysis of Within-Test Position Results

Bratko-Kopec Test

#	Age	Ratings	Name/Links	1	2	3	4	5	6	7	8	9	10	11	12
1	11	688	Adam Bachrach	0	0	0	0	0	1	0	0	0	0	0	0
2	12	1365	Andrew Bakker	0	1	0	1/3	0	0	0	0	0	0	0	0
3	16	1455	Brett Koonce	1	1	1/2	1	1	1	0	0	0	0	0	1
4	12	1373	David Baldwin	0	1	0	1	1	1/2	1	1	0	1	1	1
5	15	1262	Ian MacKenzie	0	1/4	1	1	1/4	0	0	0	0	1	0	1
6	14	1318	Isaac Marnik	0	1	0	1/3	0	0	0	0	0	0	1/2	1
7	16	973	Matt Blaine	0	0	0	0	1	0	0	0	0	0	1/2	0
8	11	1409	Matthew Brumberg	0	0	1/4	1	0	1/4	0	0	0	1/2	1	1
9	11	668	Michael Del Priore	0	0	1/2	0	0	0	0	0	0	0	1/2	1/3
10	9	1203	Nils Wernerfelt	0	1/4	0	0	0	0	0	0	0	0	0	1
11	16	1380	Samuel McHoul	1	0	0	0	0	1/3	1/3	0	0	1	0	1/2
12	12	574	Steven D.Bruestle	0	1	1	0	0	0	0	0	0	1	0	0
13	47	1386	Dwight McMahon	0	0	1/2	0	0	0	0	0	0	0	0	1
14	44	1468	Franklin Herman	1	1	0	1	0	1	0	1	0	0	1	1
15	18	1750	Tim Poole	1	1/3	0	1/2	0	1	1	1	1	1	0	1
16	13	1519	Vlad Vainberg	1	1	0	0	1	0	0	0	0	1/2	1/2	1
17	A	1800	Edward Strick	1	1	0	1	1	1	0	0	0	0	1/2	1
18	A	1750	David Le Clair	1	0	0	1	0	1/3	0	1	0	0	1	0
19	10	1050	Elina Kats	1	0	0	1	1/2	1/2	0	0	0	0	1	0
20	A	1414	Gino Malpartida	0	1/2	0	1	0	0	0	0	0	0	1	1
21	A	1750~	Jeff Schwartz	1	0	0	1	0	1/2	0	0	0	0	1	1
22	A	1500~	Ken Warwick	1	0	0	1	1/3	0	0	0	1/4	1	1	0
23	A	1871	Pat Deboris	1	1/3	0	1/2	1	1	1	1	1	1	1	1
24	A	?	Sorrice	1	1/2	1/2	1	0	1/2	0	1	0	0	1	1
25	A	1550	Thomas Felle	0	0	0	1	1	1	1/3	1/2	0	1	1	0
26	A	1600	Dave Mamula	0	0	0	1	0	0	0	0	1/2	0	1	1
27	A	1850	David Baer	0	0	0	1	0	1/2	0	0	0	0	1	1
28	A	1686	Julian Grafa	1	0	0	1	1	1	0	0	0	0	1	1
29	A	1600~	Jack Miller	0	0	0	0	0	1	0	0	0	1	1	1/2
30	18	1609	Jeremy Kallen	0	0	0	1	0	0	1/2	1/4	1/2	0	1/2	1
31	A	2000~	Michael Mansfield	1	0	0	1	1	1	0	0	0	0	1	1
32	A	1300~	Norman Nippell	0	0	0	0	0	1/3	0	0	0	1	0	1
		Total # of Correct Answers		14	14	7	22	12	19	6	8	5	12	22	24
		Total # of Wrong Answers		18	18	25	10	20	13	26	24	27	20	10	8

Question #		1	2	3	4	5	6	7	8	9	10	11
Tactical / Lever	Tactical	Lever	Lever	Lever	Tactical	Lever	Tactical	Lever	Lever	Tactical	Lever	Tactical
Sum of Scores per question	14	10 1/6	4 1/4	19 7/3	10	13 3/4	4 1/6	6 3/4	3 1/4	11	19	22 1/3
Percentile Of Right Answers	44%	44%	22%	69%	38%	59%	19%	25%	16%	38%	69%	75%
Average of Score per Questions	4/9	1/3	1/8	3/5	1/3	3/7	1/8	1/5	1/9	1/3	3/5	2/3

Sum of Lever Questions	119 3/4		Total # of Right on Lever	154
Average of Lever Questions	1/3			
Percentile of Lever Questions	40%		Total # of Wrong on lever	230
Sum of Tactical Questions	112		Total # of Right on Tactical	123
Average of Tactical Questions	2/7			
Percentile of Tactical Questions	32%		Total # of Wrong on Tactical	261

* Stands for an Adult

13	14	15	16	17	18	19	20	21	22	23	24		Total Correct	Total Wrong	Score
0	0	0	0	1/3	0	0	1/4	0	1	0	1/3		5	19	3
1/2	0	0	0	0	0	0	0	1	0	0	0		4	20	2 5/6
0	1	0	0	0	0	0	0	0	0	0	0		8	16	7 1/2
1/2	1	1	0	1	0	0	1/2	0	0	0	1		15	9	13 1/2
0	1	0	0	0	0	0	0	0	1/3	0	1/4		9	15	6
1	0	1/2	0	0	0	0	1/3	0	0	0	0		7	17	4 2/3
1	0	0	0	0	0	0	0	0	0	0	0		3	21	2 1/2
0	0	0	0	0	0	0	0	1	0	1/3	1		9	15	6 1/3
0	0	0	0	0	0	0	0	0	0	0	0		3	21	1 1/3
0	0	0	0	0	0	0	0	0	0	1	0		3	21	2 1/4
0	1/3	0	0	0	0	1	0	0	0	1/2	0		8	16	5
0	0	0	0	0	0	0	0	0	0	0	0		3	21	3
0	0	0	0	0	0	0	0	0	0	1/2	0		3	21	2
0	0	0	0	1	0	0	1/3	1	0	0	1		11	13	10 1/3
1/2	1	1	1	0	1	1	0	1	1	0	1		18	6	16 1/3
0	0	1	1	0	0	0	1/3	1/2	0	0	1		11	13	8 5/6
1	0	1	0	1	0	0	1/3	1	1	0	1		14	10	12 5/6
1	1	0	0	1	0	0	1	1	0	0	1		11	13	10 1/3
0	1	1	0	0	0	0	0	1	0	0	1/3		9	15	7 1/3
1	0	0	1/2	0	0	0	1	0	0	0	1		8	16	7
0	0	0	1	0	0	0	0	1/3	0	0	0		7	17	5 5/6
1/2	0	0	0	1	0	0	0	1/2	1	0	1/2		11	13	8
1	1	1	1	1	0	1	1	1	0	1	1		21	3	19 5/6
0	1	1	1	0	0	0	0	1	0	0	0		12	12	10 1/2
0	0	1	0	0	0	1	0	1	1	0	0		11	13	9 5/6
0	0	0	0	0	0	0	0	0	0	0	1		5	19	4 1/2
0	0	1	0	0	0	0	0	0	0	0	0		5	19	4 1/2
0	0	0	1	1/2	0	1/2	0	1	0	1	1		12	12	11
0	0	0	0	1/3	0	0	1/3	0	0	0	1/4		7	17	4 3/7
1	0	0	0	0	0	0	0	0	0	1/3	1		9	15	6
0	1	0	1	1	0	0	1	1	0	0	1		12	12	12
0	0	0	0	0	0	0	0	0	0	0	0		3	21	2 1/3
11	10	10	8	10	1	5	11	15	6	7	18				
21	22	22	24	22	31	27	21	17	26	25	14				

12	13	14	15	16	17	18	19	20	21	22	23	24
Lever	Tactical	Tactical	Tactical	Lever	Tactical	Tactical	Lever	Tactical	Tactical	Lever	Lever	
9	9 1/3	9 1/2	7 1/2	8 1/6	1	4 1/2	6 2/5	13 1/3	5 1/3	4 2/3	14 2/3	
34%	31%	31%	25%	31%	3%	16%	34%	47%	19%	22%	56%	
2/7	2/7	2/7	1/4	1/4	0	1/7	1/5	2/5	1/6	1/7	1/2	

The preceding table represents a detailed analysis of 32 subjects' performance on the Bratko-Kopec Test over several years. Since 1982 we have tested over 300 people on the "BK-Test" as it is known.

Unfortunately we cannot report all the results here, but overall we can confirm that the performance results have continued to be very reliable, with regard to rating and in terms of suggesting where a player's strengths and weaknesses lie with regard to tactics and strategical play (levers here).

We are very grateful to Mr. Von Agojo who collected, organized and analyzed the above data for his CIS 60.1 (Senior) project in Computer Science at Brooklyn College (Fall, 2001). This has enabled us to look at some of the performance results for these subjects whose ratings range from expert (2000) to beginner (under 1000) "under a microscope." For example, based on our experience (and intuition) we had ranked as "very hard" positions 7, 18, 22, and 23 of the BK-Test, assigning each of them a difficulty level (page 24) of 4.

Indeed, subjects scored an overall performance (by percentage) on these four positions, of 19 (T), 18 (T), 19 (L) and 22 (T), (some of the lowest percentage scores), on the four positions as shown above. However, subjects also had a low (under 30%) performance score on positions 3 (L, 22), 8 (L, 25), 9 (L, 16), 16 (T, 25), and 19 (T, 16). We should note that Mr. Agojo's method of assigning an equal weight to correct choices (which are possibly 2nd, 3rd, or 4th choices), for a given position, may be questioned. Using these equal weights, he derives his percentages — but this approach may raise doubts, since 2nd , 3rd or 4th choices should not be assigned equal probabilities in deriving the overall correctness score for a position.

Appendix 9

Rating Improvement with Testing

This may be the most remarkable result of all. It shows that simply by collecting a sample selection of rated players who attended Kopec's Chess Camp in 2001 and who were tested at the Camp, we see significant rating improvements. Analysis of the data using the Wilcoxin signed ranks matched pairs statistic (T) indicates that it is very unlikely that these results (rating improvements) could have occurred by chance. Still it is important to point out that most of the rating improvement occurs with Juniors. Juniors tend to be active players and often have coaching which undoubtedly contributes to their improvement. Nontheless, we believe that testing and the postmortem analysis of the test results does lead to a significant increase in knowledge and improvement. We would like to acknowledge Ms. Florette Cohen for performing the Wilcoxin Test on this data.

Name	June 2001 Rating	December 2001 Rating	Age	Difference/ change	Rank
Adam McIntosh	1787	1800	14	13	3
A J Rice	1708	1725	11	17	4
Amrit Gupta	1270	1556	13	286	16
Dan Callan	Unrated	Unrated	Adult	0	
Daniel Fine	1478	1553	14	75	8
Daniel Gordon	1643	1673	14	30	6
Daniel Judd	1361	1551	10	190	15
George Gerolimatos	975	921	Adult	-54	-1
Ian Harris	1174	1358	14	184	14
Jake Vogel	1375	1681	15	306	17
Mackenzie Molner	1798	1892	13	94	10
Matthew Klegon	1349	1447	12	98	12
Matthew Di Pasquale	1240	1329	15	89	9
Michael Cambareri	1539	1646	10	107	13
Ron Schmid	1336	1373	Adult	37	7
Sean Finn	1809	1772	13	-37	-2
Thomas Bhame	1489	1489	Adult	0	
Tyler McIntosh	1497	1516	11	19	5
Jason Mielke	1498	1594	12	96	11

Bibliography

Alburt, Lev and Roman Pelts. *Comprehensive Chess Course, Vol. II.* Chess Information Research Center, New York, NY, 1986.

Averbakh, Yuri. *Queen and Pawn Endings*. Batsford, 1975.

Averbakh, Yuri. *Rook v. Minor Piece Endings*. Batsford, 1978.

Clarke, Michael (Editor). *Advances in Computer Chess I*, 1977.

Clarke, Michael (Editor). *Advances in Computer Chess II*, 1980.

Euwe, Max. *Meet the Masters.* Sir Isaac Pitman & Sons, Ltd. London, 1940.

Fine, Reuben. *Basic Chess Endings.* McKay, 1941.

Fischer, Bobby. *Bobby Fischer Teaches Chess.* Basic Systems, Inc., 1966.

Hays, Lou. *Winning Chess Tactics for Juniors*. Hays Publishing, 1994.

Hort, Vlastimil and Vlastimil Jansa. *The Best Move*. RHM Press, New York, 1980.

Kmoch, Hans. *Pawn Power in Chess*. McKay, 1959.

Kopec, Danny; Geoffrey Chandler, Chris Morrison, Nigel Davies and Ian Mullen. *Mastering Chess: A Course in 21 Lessons.* Pergamon Press, 1985. Revised, Cadogan, 1994.

Matanovic, Aleksandar (Editor). *Chess Informant 18*, 1975.

Matanovic, Aleksandar (Editor). *Chess Informant 26*, 1978.

Pachman, Ludek. *Modern Chess Tactics*. Routledge & Kegan Paul. London, 1973.

Portisch, Lajos and Balazs Sarkozy. *600 Endings*. Sport, Budapest, 1976.

Pritchett, Craig and Kopec, Danny. *Best Games of the Young Grand-masters*. Bell & Hyman Ltd., 1980.

Smyslov, Vasily and Grigory Levenfish. *Rook Endings*. Batsford, 1978.

References, 2002 Edition

References (in Reverse Chronological Order)

Kopec, D. and Prichett, C. (2002), *World Chess Tiltle Contenders and Their Styles*, Dover, Mineola, NY.

Kopec, D. and Terrie, H., (1997) *Test, Evaluate, and Improve Your Chess: a Knowledge-Based Approach*, Hypermodern Press, San Francisco.

Berliner, H., Kopec, D. and Ed Northam, (1991) *A Taxonomy of Concepts for Evaluating Chess Strength: examples from two difficult categories*. in *Advances in Computer Chess 6*, (ed. Don Beal), Ellis Horwood, Chichester, England, pp. 179-91

Berliner, H., Kopec, D. and Northam, E.) (1990) *A Taxonomy of Concepts for Evaluating Chess Strength*, Proceedings of SUPERCOMPUTING '90 , N.Y.C., New York, November 15-17, pp. 336-43.

Kopec, D., Newborn, M. and Yu, W., (1985). *Experiments in Chess Cognition. In Advances in Computer Chess 4* (ed. D. Beal) Pergamon Press, Oxford, England.

Kopec, D. and Bratko, I. (1982). *The Bratko-Kopec Experiment: A test for comparison of human and computer performance in chess*. In *Advances in Computer Chess 3*, (ed. M.R.B. Clarke). Pergamon Press, Oxford, England.

Bratko, I., Michie, D. and Kopec, D. (1978). *Pattern-based representation of chess endgame knowledge*. Computer Journal, 21(2), pp. 149-53.

Huberman, Barbara, Stanford University, Ph.D. Thesis, 1969.

Kmoch, Hans, *Pawn Power in Chess*, David McKay, 1959.

Index of Position Categories

Chapter 1: New Positions Test

Chapter 2: The Camp Test

Eight positions each in the Opening, Middlegame and Endgame

50. W (CT #2) Middlegame. Attacking lever
51. B (CT #3) Opening. Pirc-Austrian: know your counter play
52. W (CT #4) Middlegame. Mobilize kingside majority
53. W (CT #5) Opening. French Winawer: overloaded Black queen
54. W (CT #6) Middlegame. Kingside lever to provoke leucopenia
55. B (CT #7) Ending. Decoy, undermining, promotion tactics
56. W (CT #8) Middlegame. Original version of classic bishop sacrifice
57. W (CT #9) Opening. Ruy Lopez/Schliemann Variation: piece sacrifice for attack
58. B (CT #10) Middlegame. Bring in the forces for wrap-up (rook lift)
59. W (CT #11) Ending. Active king in rook and pawn ending.
60. B (CT #12) Opening. Pirc-Austrian: queen sacrifice gives counterplay to draw
61. W (CT #13) Middlegame. Add fuel to the fire, back rank and forks
62. W (CT #14) Ending. Enforce undoubling lever
63. W (CT #15) Opening. Modern Benoni: specific knowledge necessary
64. B (CT #16) Middlegame. Close the position to the two bishops
65. B (CT #17) Opening. French Winawer with Qg4, best defensive try
66. W (CT #18) Ending. King and pawn ending, triangulation
67. B (CT #19) Opening. Ruy Lopez/Exchange Variation: specific knowledge necessary
68. W (CT #20) Ending. Maximum file distance and rank for opposition.
69. W (CT #21) Middlegame. Browne's sacrificial melee
70. B (CT #22) Ending. Active rook behind passed pawn
71. B (CT #23) Opening. Nimzo-Indian Defense/Classical Variation: specific knowledge needed
72. W (CT #24) Ending. Pin, pawn play prevents liberation

Chapter 3: The Rook and Pawn Test

	Side to Move		Category	Better
73.	W	(RP #1)	1	Better rook, pawns, king
74.	W	(RP #2)	2	Better rook, pawns
75.	W	(RP #3)	3	Better pawns, king
76.	W	(RP #4)	4	Better rook, king
77.	W	(RP #5)	5	Better rook
78.	W	(RP #6)	6	Better pawns
79.	W	(RP #7)	7	Better king
80.	W	(RP #8)	6	Better pawns
81.	W	(RP #9)	7	Better king
82.	B	(RP #10)	0	No advantage
83.	W	(RP #11)	1	Better rook, pawns, king
84.	B	(RP #12)	2	Better rook, pawns
85.	B	(RP #13)	3	Better pawns, king
86.	W	(RP #14)	4	Better rook, king
87.	W	(RP #15)	5	Better rook
88.	B	(RP #16)	6	Better pawns
89.	W	(RP #17)	7	Better king
90.	W	(RP #18)	6	Better pawns
91.	B	(RP #19)	0	No advantage
92.	B	(RP #20)	0	No advantage
93.	W	(RP #21)	1	Better rook, pawns, king
94.	W	(RP #22)	2	Better rook, pawns
95.	W	(RP #23)	3	Better pawns, king
96.	W	(RP #24)	4	Better, rook, king
97.	W	(RP #25)	5	Better rook
98.	W	(RP #26)	2	Better rook, pawns
99.	W	(RP #27)	7	Better king
100.	B	(RP #28)	4	Better rook, king
101.	W	(RP #29)	2	Better rook, pawns
102.	B	(RP #30)	0	No advantage
103.	B	(RP #31)	2	Better rook, pawns
104.	B	(RP #32)	1	Better rook, pawns, king
105.	W	(RP #33)	3	Better pawns, king
106.	W	(RP #34)	4	Better rook, king
107.	W	(RP #35)	5	Better rook

Chapter 4: The Other Endings Test

108. W   (OE #1)   Two bishops vs. bishop and knight; regroup to activate and dominate

109. W   (OE #2)   Rook and bishop vs. rook and knight; maximize rook activity, probe weaknesses

110. B   (OE #3)   Rook and bishop vs. rook and knight; avoid simplification to known deficits

111. W   (OE #4)   Queen and Pawn ending; getting a passed pawn is key

112. W   (OE #5)   Bishop vs. knight; head for *zugzwang*

113. W   (OE #6)   Rook vs. bishop and pawns; must activate passed pawn and king

114. B   (OE #7)   Bishop vs. bishop (same color); bad bishop, lever, pawns on same color

115. B   (OE #8)   Rook vs. knight (no pawns); draw by repetition check, king kept at bay

116. B   (OE #9)   Double rook ending; must activate and double rooks on 7th

117. W   (OE #10) Knight vs. bad bishop; better king, lever to force entry

118. B   (OE #11) Rook vs. bishop (no pawns); avoid mate

119. W   (OE #12) Bishop vs. bishop (opposite color); trade pawns, stalemate trick

120. B   (OE #13) King and pawn ending; activate king, "pawn island" theory

121. W   (OE #14) Knight vs. knight; fundamental lever

122. B   (OE #15) Bishop vs. bishop (opposite color); separated passed pawns beat connected

123. W   (OE #16) King and pawn ending; dominant king, space, *zugzwang*

124. W   (OE #17) Two bishops vs. bishop and knight; probe to open position

125. W   (OE #18) King and pawn ending; chain lever

126. W   (OE #19) Knight vs. knight; better knight, space: convert to passed pawn

127. W   (OE #20) Bishop vs. knight; *zugzwang* for domination

128. W   (OE #21) Bishop vs. bishop (same color); pawns fixed on color of bishop, better king

Chapter 5: The Novice Test

(Eight positions each in the Opening, Middlegame and Endgame)

Chapter 6: The Intermediate Test

(Eight positions each in the Opening, Middlegame and Endgame)

Acknowledgments

I would like to take this opportunity to acknowledge those who have made this book possible. First, Professor Ivan Bratko, of the Josef Stefan Institute in Ljubljana for helping me to produce the original Bratko-Kopec Test. Second, Professor Donald Michie for being supportive of this kind of research in his lab during my six years there. Third, Professor Monty Newborn of McGill University and the chessplayers in Montreal who supported the research entitled "Experiments in Chess Cognition" leading to the New Positions Test.

I would also like to thank all the people and programs that have taken our tests over the years. They have contributed greatly to the development of our tests. We are especially grateful to the computer chess programmers who recognized the Bratko-Kopec Test as the standard test for many years. None of this work would have occurred without the cooperation of literally hundreds of enthusiastic chessplayers all over the world for over 20 years.

I have greatly appreciated the continuing encouragement of my friends and colleagues Professors George Markowsky and Tony Marsland, as well as Dr. Hans Berliner and Professor Ed Northam for collaborating with me on the development of a "Taxonomy of Chess Concepts" which was the seed for our more recent tests. My Chairman at the U.S. Coast Guard Academy, Professor Richard Close also deserves acknowledgment for viewing this kind of work positively.

Co-author Hal Terrie, who has been a lifelong friend and supporter and deserves special recognition. Without Hal, this book would probably still not be in print, and if printed, would have been lacking in many ways. Hal added the NOVTEST and took care of many necessary details in producing a consistent and thorough effort. He has been a facilitator who has kept the project moving forward despite my occasionally fiery temper. In a manner of speaking, he "stayed in the kitchen, despite the heat."

FM Jim Eade, the publisher, of our first edition (1997) who some 20 years ago saw the value of my knowledge-based approach to chess and had the vision to see the importance of this book, encouraged us to include that approach in all aspects of the work. M.L. Rantala was a dedicated and concerned editor (of the first edition) who attended to all the necessary aspects of making this book as versatile and accurate as possible.

I would like to acknowledge my wife Sylvia, son David, and stepson Oliver for having the patience to allow this work to be completed.

—Danny Kopec, 1995

We would like to thank all those who have helped us improve this new edition by participating in our tests since the publication of the first edition.

First, we must thank USCF Executive Director for ensuring that this book is a USCF publication. I (DK) would also like to thank Frank and Dr. Tim Redman for inviting me to The Koltanowsky Memorial Conference on Chess and Education (Dallas, Texas, Dec. 12-14, 2001) as well as Brooklyn College for its support in enabling me to participate in this Conference. I would also like to thank Von R. Agojo for assistance with data preparation for Appendices, and Mr. Jim Bovy for securing us a Compaq Corporation Grant in 2001.

Finally, and by no means in the least, we would like to thank Jamie Anson, and her assistants (especially Jean Bernice, Claudia Bonforte, Cathy Garone, Paula Helmeset and Michelle Stowe) for the book design and typography. The editorial directorship of this 2nd edition by Glenn Petersen with whom we have had the pleasure and honor of working with for over 10 years as editor of *Chess Life*, brings us great security that we have produced a valuable work. It was Glenn's idea to repeat the test positions with the solutions. And we would like to acknowledge Jack Edelson for his assistance with analysis.

—Danny Kopec, 2002

About The Authors

Danny Kopec

Danny Kopec is one of the most talented home-bred U.S. players. Dr. Kopec was New York High School Champion at 14, National Master at 17, Scottish Champion in 1980, 2nd-equal in the Canadian Closed in 1984, and was awarded the International Master title in 1985. He is an active player, journalist, writer, chess educator and scholar. His competitive results with top-flight chess professionals have always been remarkable. He has also delivered many chess courses and lectures, and has developed five highly acclaimed instructional videos as well as authored or co-authored five chess books. His Kopec's Chess Camp, has become world renowned. (www.kopecchess.com)

In parallel with his chess career, Dr. Kopec has pursued an academic career in computer science concentrating on artificial intelligence. For more than 20 years, Kopec has been testing and evaluating hundreds of chessplayers in the U.K., Canada, and U.S. in order to quantify their overall chess strength, their specific deficiencies and definite abilities. In bridging his chess and academic interests, Kopec has developed a reputation as perhaps the world's greatest exponent of chess knowledge. This book represents a large portion of Dr. Kopec's overall efforts to help chessplayers understand and achieve the knowledge necessary to achieve chess mastery.

Hal Terrie is a Life and Correspondence Master whose tournament career spans many years, during which he has defeated and drawn a number of titled players. A well-known New England chess promoter and tournament organizer, he has organized and directed scores of tournaments, including two New England Championships. He has served for seven years as Associate Director of Kopec's Chess Camp. He is also a private instructor, who has twice coached scholastic teams to first place finishes, and has had several students who appeared on top 50 rating lists for their age group.

Hal Terrie

SAY YES TO OUR CHILDREN!

Chess is a wonderful game that can help children:
✳ Develop mental discipline ✳ Develop analytical skills
✳ Develop strategic thinking skills ✳ Do better in school
✳ And much more ...

It is estimated that there are more than 30 million children who play chess in America. This number is growing. In a recent survey, it shows that there are more children playing chess than playing other major sports such as baseball, football, basketball, hockey, etc. But, our children need guidance and direction, and there are countless children who do not even have this opportunity at all!

THE U.S. CHESS TRUST'S MISSION
IS TO PROVIDE CHESS EDUCATION FOR AMERICA!

Its arm extends to every state in the nation, providing educational tools to people of all ages.
The Trust provides: ■ *FREE* chess equipment to schools, hospitals, clubs, etc.
■ Full or partial scholarships ■ *FREE* memberships to needy children
■ Training materials for teachers and coaches ■ And, a lot more ...

COMBINED FEDERAL CAMPAIG
COMBINED FEDERAL CAMPAIGN

WITHOUT YOUR DONATIONS, WE DON'T EXIST!
Please be generous and support the U.S. Chess Trust.
Please give our children and others this wonderful opportunity.

Please ☑1115

All donations to the Chess Trust are tax-deductible.

U.S. Chess Trust
www.uschess.org
1-800-388-KING
(5464)

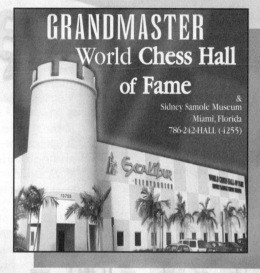

About the U.S. Chess Federation

❖ The United States Chess Federation, founded in 1939, serves as the governing body of chess in the United States and is devoted to extending the role of chess in American society. It promotes the study and knowledge of the game of chess, for its own sake as an art and enjoyment, and as a means for the improvement of society. The USCF is a not-for-profit membership organization, with nearly 90,000 members, and more than 2,300 USCF-affiliated chess clubs.

❖ The U.S. Chess Trust, a 501(c)(3) charitable trust administered by the USCF, supports chess programs for schools, veterans, hospitals, and prisons nationwide.

❖ The USCF sanctions thousands of chess tournaments, rates half a million games each year, and organizes national and international championship events. As a not-for-profit membership organization, the USCF applies its revenue to services and programs benefitting its members and chess in America.

❖ The USCF was founded in 1939 and grew steadily until 1972, when membership doubled as a result of the surge of interest in chess linked to the popularity of World Champion Bobby Fischer. The USCF's regular monthly publication, *Chess Life*, is distributed nationally to a readership in excess of 250,000.

❖ The USCF sanctions more than 40 national championship events, including: the U.S. Championship, and the U.S. Amateur, U.S. Junior and U.S. Senior Championships. The USCF sponsors the National Scholastic Championships (Elementary, Junior High, and High School) each of which annually draws thousands of players. The USCF also sponsors American participation in international events such as World Chess Olympiads and World Championship cycles. Fifty of the world's grandmasters live in the United States. The U.S. Chess Champion is Alex Shabalov, and the U.S. Women's Champion is Anna Hahn.

❖ The USCF rating system, developed in the early 1960s by statisticians Arpad Elo and Kenneth Harkness, rates the performance of chessplayers in officially sanctioned tournaments. Ratings range from 100 to 2800, with an average of about 1300.

www.uschess.org

U.S. CHESS FEDERATION
800.388.KING(5464) · 845.562.8350 · Fax 845.561.CHES (2437)
3054 US ROUTE 9W, NEW WINDSOR, NY 12553 · www.uschess.org

Kopec's Chess Camps 2003

June 28-29
WORLD OPEN CLINIC
Two days testing, instruction and analysis at
World Open hotel in Philadelphia, from clinic's Master staff.

July 6-13 or 13-20
THE LAWRENCEVILLE SCHOOL
LAWRENCEVILLE, NJ (NEAR PRINCETON)
COMBINED SCHEDULES
✳ Two-week option (7/6-20)
✳ Ten-day option (7/6-17)
✳ Short-Week Option (7/14-17)
✳ Other schedules possible as well.
Call or check our website for full details.
*"FIRST-RATE INSTRUCTION IN A
FIRST-RATE SETTING"*

❖ Diverse Commuter
 and Boarding Program
❖ Great Location, Superb
 Facilities in Beautiful Setting
❖ TENNIS, Group instruction
❖ Use of latest Computer/
 Database Technology

**Superb
Facilities!**
*Boarding or commuter
options available*

*For More Information Call (After 6:00 pm or week-
ends): (516) 867- 4031; if busy call (603) 668-8368,
E-mail: IM Danny Kopec: Drk2501@aol.com or Hal
Terrie: halterrie@worldnet.att.net • Visit Our Web
Site: www.kopecchess.com • Or Write : Kopec Chess
Services, 34 East Webster St., Merrick, NY 11566*

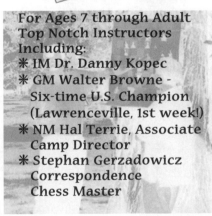

For Ages 7 through Adult
Top Notch Instructors
Including:
✳ IM Dr. Danny Kopec
✳ GM Walter Browne -
 Six-time U.S. Champion
 (Lawrenceville, 1st week!)
✳ NM Hal Terrie, Associate
 Camp Director
✳ Stephan Gerzadowicz
 Correspondence
 Chess Master

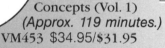

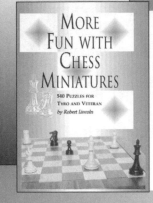